THE GUINNESS BOOK OF

Beards and Moustaches

Leslie Dunkling
and John Foley

GUINNESS PUBLISHING

PICTURE CREDITS

Associated Newspapers Ltd.
Billie Love Collection
British Museum
Hulton Picture Library
London Features International Ltd.
London Weekend Television
Mary Evans
National Film Archive, London
Popperfoto
Scott Downie
Syndication International

Special thanks to: J. Stevens Cox, FSA for kind permission to use illustrations from
An Illustrated Dictionary of Hairdressing and Wigmaking and to The Post Office for the use
of the Edward Lear stamp.

Front cover artwork by Rob Heesom
Text artwork on p. 40/41 and 111 by Peter Bull
Line drawings: p. 81, 93 from *A Book of Nonsense* by Edward Lear, 1846; p. 82 from *More
Nonsense, Pictures, Rhymes, Botany, etc.* (1872).
Picture of Edward Sedman on p. 106/107 courtesy of Sky Television.

Editor: Beatrice Frei
Picture Editor: Alex Goldberg
Design and Layout: Michael Morey

© Leslie Dunkling, John Foley and Guinness Publishing Ltd, 1990

Published in Great Britain by Guinness Publishing Ltd,
33 London Road, Enfield, Middlesex

Typeset in Palatino by Ace Filmsetting Ltd, Frome, Somerset
Printed and bound in Great Britain by The Bath Press, Bath

'Guinness' is a registered trade mark of Guinness Superlatives Ltd

British Library Cataloguing in Publication Data
Dunkling, Leslie, 1935–
   Guinness book of beards & moustaches.
   1. Men. Beards & moustaches
   I. Title II. Foley, John
   391'.5

   ISBN 0-85112-906-4

Front Cover: Left to right; top to bottom *Chin-beard, Franz Josef, Goatee, Lincolnic, Bush,
Pique-devant, Designer stubble, Full, Polar beaver, Handlebar, Forked, Mephistopheles, Mexican,
Assyrian, Screw, Toothbrush, Sideburns, Walrus.*

Leslie Dunkling has indulged in beard and moustache spotting for 20 years while commuting to his job with the BBC World Service. He has thought about growing some personal face fungus, but has never got past the undesigned-weekend-stubble stage. He lives in Thames Ditton, near Hampton Court, once the home of the handsomely-bearded Henry VIII.

John Foley has worked extensively as an actor throughout Britain and the USA with a variety of 'face furnishings', either false or home-grown. He first became interested in pogonology whilst collaborating with Leslie Dunkling on a radio series for BBC English where he was a member of the repertory company. Now freelance, he divides his time between acting, broadcasting, and writing which includes regular adaptations and features for BBC World Service and storylining for Disney comics.

Contents

Introduction

This is a book about beards and moustaches (not to mention the occasional side-whiskers) in all their glory. It is a book about face fungus long and short, ancient and modern, true and false, religious and secular, historical and royal. You will read about beard games and beard jokes, discover why men grow them or decide not to grow them, why they are sometimes not allowed to grow them, what happens to beards and moustaches once they have been grown, why some men decide to shave them off. We will tell you what women think of them, what scientists and medical men have discovered about them. In this miniature encyclopaedia of the subject we will show you different beard and moustache styles with which to experiment, and provide you with a comprehensive beard, moustache and whiskers glossary.

At the moment, clean-shaven male faces constitute the norm. By definition, those who sport a beard or moustache are abnormal. Rubbish, they would say, there are dozens of reasons why a man should have a beard or moustache. Let us begin, then, by allowing them to state their case.

1 *All those in favour . . .*

In this chapter some of the arguments that have been advanced in favour of beards are presented. It is surprising how extensive (and convincing) the list is. It is such a long chapter that if you have not got a beard, but are thinking of growing one, you might as well start now. By the time you get to the end you will be well on the way.

Maybe you are worried about what your friends and relations might say if you decide to grow a beard? Forget them, and do your own thing. Or, as a 19th-century writer expressed it: 'Let him who assumes the beard plant himself on what he conceives the sense and right of the matter; his moral courage will then sustain him until his friends, who may now amuse themselves at his expense, shall esteem him for his brave fidelity to his convictions.'

A bearded acquaintance of ours put it a different way: 'A beard is an asset more often than not. It gives strength to a face. Women are aroused by a beard.'

He may well be right. Ray Bull, author of a book on the social psychology of appearance, says that surveys have shown that men with beards are thought to be more masculine, independent, strong, mature and sophisticated. 'So men who grow them either have those qualities or hope to acquire them along with their hairier appearance.'

POGONOLOGY AND PUBERTY

No one would argue with Mr Bull if he said that young men who are trying to grow a beard hope to acquire those qualities. Just as a young girl might study herself in the bathroom mirror, looking for evidence that she is developing into a woman, so a youth is likely to search for the first signs of a moustache or beard, which will label him as a man. In Victorian times, when men were more generally bearded, the first bristles were perhaps even more important than they are today. Charles Dickens pokes gentle fun at young men who are experiencing the agonising waiting period in the character of Fledgeby. In *Our Mutual Friend* he is described as follows: 'an awkward, sandy-haired, small-eyed youth, and prone to self-examination in the articles of whisker and moustache. While feeling for the

Charles Dickens (1812–70) with a chin-beard.

whisker that he anxiously expected, Fledgeby underwent remarkable fluctuations of spirits, ranging along the whole scale from confidence to despair. There were times when he started, as exclaiming, "By Jupiter, here it is at last!" There were other times when, being equally depressed, he would be seen to shake his head, and give up hope. To see him at those periods leaning on a chimney piece, like as on an urn containing the ashes of his ambition, with the cheek that would not sprout, upon the hand on which that cheek had forced conviction, was a distressing sight.'

Later in the novel, Dickens returns to the theme. 'All rise. The ladies go upstairs. The gentlemen soon saunter after them. Fledgeby has devoted the interval to taking an observation of Boots's whiskers, Brewer's whiskers, and Lammle's whiskers, and considering which pattern of whisker he would prefer to produce out of himself by friction, if the genie of his cheek would only answer to his rubbing.'

Another 19th-century writer makes a similar comment. *Flowers From a Persian Garden* (1890), by W A Clouston, has a chapter on 'The Beards of Our Fathers'. It begins: 'Among the harmless foibles of adolescence which contribute to the quiet amusement of folks of mature years is the eager desire of youths to have their smooth faces adorned with that "noble" distinction of manhood — a beard. And no wonder. For should a clever lad venture to express opinions contrary to those of his elders present, is he not at once snubbed by being called a "beardless boy"?'

Things have changed a bit since the 19th century, and young men are less often snubbed when they venture an opinion. Nor are they called 'beardless boys' so often: not surprisingly when one considers that most older men these days are beardless themselves. The 'beardless boy' put-down, though, was once very common. One of those stories which gets attached to a different person every time it is told is sometimes linked with the young Augustus Keppel, later Viscount Admiral Keppel, commander-in-chief of the British Navy in the late 18th century. Keppel is said to have been sent as an emissary to the Governor of Algiers, with

instructions to tell that dignitary to stop his piratical activities.

The Governor was not impressed with the 'beardless boy' who had come to lecture him, and questioned the wisdom of the King of England in sending someone so young. 'Had my master supposed that wisdom was measured by the length of the beard, he would have sent your Excellency a he-goat,' said Keppel. The remark supposedly enraged the Governor, who threatened Keppel with instant death. The young man is said to have indicated the British naval squadron which was anchored in the bay and remarked that there were probably enough Englishmen there to make a glorious funeral pyre for him. The Governor saw the point, and Keppel departed with due dignity.

Anyway, one basic reason for growing a beard is to prove to oneself and to the world that one is now a man. This is commonly said, but John Sparrow has pointed out that this is not necessarily the case today. A beard on a young man is often accompanied by long curly hair, worn over the shoulder like a girl's. He quotes an Oxford don who complains that it has been years since he has seen the back of a young man's neck.

Another reason a young man grows a beard is to make himself look older, or more mature. This seems quite a sensible idea. The writer Sir Compton Mackenzie once said that when a man first grows a beard, everyone tells him that he is looking much older. As the years go by, however, and the beard remains the same, everyone says that he does not seem to age at all. He could have added that there may come a time when removal of the beard will make everyone say how much younger he looks — no bad thing when he has reached middle age.

STUBBLE TROUBLE

It is worth making the point that it is not just young men who sometimes find it difficult to grow a beard. Most men have probably at one time or another toyed with the idea of growing one, but it is not that easy to experiment. Normal life has to continue while the beard is growing, which means that for a period of at least three weeks, the man concerned will simply look unshaven rather than bearded. 'Like all other excellent things,' said a magazine writer in the 1890s, 'except mushrooms, the beard does not spring up in a single night. In its transitional stage, it is not altogether a thing of beauty. The man then feels that he is hardly fit for the society of his fellow creatures. He has many humiliating moments to endure ere the time of his dignity has come.'

First experiments with a beard are therefore often carried out in the summer, when the man concerned is on vacation, but it is a race against time. Will the beard have become a true beard before the normal daily round is resumed? If it is still a stubbly mess and

Singer and honorary knight, Bob Geldof, making stubble fashionable in the 1980s.

has to be removed, what will be the effect on one's sun-tanned face? Returning to the office with patches of blotchy skin on one's cheeks is not a happy prospect. The net result of all this is that for every beard that reaches full maturity, there are many more which are aborted at stubble stage. This is no doubt why designer stubble became briefly and (some would say) ridiculously fashionable in the 1980s. The much-reduced waiting period suited the mood of the times, when everyone wanted instant results.

When designer stubble was at its most fashionable height in 1985, some of those who favoured it explained why. Philip Sturgeon, an American male model, was quoted in *Time* magazine as saying: 'I feel more sexy, more virile, and it helps me get into character.' Michael

Bennett, director-choreographer of *A Chorus Line* and *Dreamgirls*, said: 'I got bored looking in the mirror. I don't think it's interpreted as being sloppy any longer. It's part of the 80s.' Actor David Keith insisted that there was a practical reason for his wearing the stubble look: 'Zits (spots). I'm 31 and I still break out when I shave.' Model Christopher Schwarz's view was that 'women find stubble very sexy. They get the sense of kissing someone adventurous. They love to rub their faces in it.'

Most commentators attributed the designer stubble phenomenon to actor Don Johnson, in his role as Detective Crockett in *Miami Vice*. The specially-developed electric razor which appeared at the

Clint Eastwood and five-day stubble.

time, one which left a two-day stubble on the face, was generally known as the Miami De-vice. Sylvester Stallone had also helped things along. Earlier, Clint Eastwood had been seen in the spaghetti westerns with a five-day stubble to accompany his cheroot, sarape and Colt Peacemaker. Significantly, the trend for designer stubble is said to have begun in Italy some years before it reached Britain and the US.

Long before the designer stubble phenomenon, David Webb, who played as a defender for Queen's Park Rangers football club, said in 1976 that he cultivated a stubble before playing matches in Europe. The idea was to look tough, or as he expressed it: 'Just because I'm English, opposing poncy forwards know I'm going to be a hard nut. But if I can look a hard nut, too, that's another little victory won — and the game ain't even started.'

PRAGMATIC POGONOLOGY

Further arguments in favour of a real beard include those put forward in a *Times* article by Joseph Connolly in 1986:

- the saving of money that would otherwise be spent on razors, lotions and the like,
- the saving of time in not shaving — up to 60 hours a year,
- the avoidance of a stubbled face at the breakfast table,
- the avoidance of five o'clock shadow,

George Bernard Shaw (1856–1950) who once described his beard as 'so like a tuft of blanched grass that pet animals have nibbled at it'.

- the avoidance of the pain caused to a sensitive throat by 'the raspings of an electric razor',
- the avoidance of the painful stinging caused by expensive after-shave lotions.

Mr Connolly also pointed out that bearded men were not as vain as their clean-shaven friends, who spend so much time staring at themselves in the mirror every morning.

Viscount Macmillan, chairman of the publishing house of that name, once said in an interview that his beard made him look distinguished. He added: 'My wife thinks it's sexy and my children think it's hysterical.'

We must also consider the views of George Bernard Shaw. He was once approached by the advertising executive of a company manufacturing electric razors. The executive hoped to persuade Shaw to endorse the company's new product by using it to shave off his famous beard. Instead, Shaw explained why he had chosen to grow a beard. When he was about five years old, Shaw said, he had been watching his father shave himself and had asked, with childish innocence: 'Daddy, why do you shave?' His father had considered the question carefully for a full minute, silently. He had then thrown his razor out of the window, saying: 'Why the hell do I?' According to Shaw, his father never shaved again, and he himself had seen no reason to begin. One imagines that on hearing this family anecdote, the electric razor man rapidly changed the subject.

Incidentally, Michael Holroyd, in the first volume of his biography of Shaw (*The Search for Love 1856–1898*), says that later in life Shaw represented himself as the passive partner to his beard; he simply followed it wherever it went.

By a curious coincidence, another Shaw adopted a similarly passive attitude. Asked by a journalist why he wore a beard, teacher Dickin Shaw replied: 'You tell me first why everyone removes what's there. I don't grow it. It grows. Why spend hours, weeks, years scraping away if there is no real necessity?'

George Bernard Shaw was certainly fond of his beard and was not alone in that respect. 'I fondle it at all hours of the day and night: I caress it and cuddle

it,' wrote John Knight, in a *Guardian* article some years ago. He added: 'Like thatch it is warm in winter and cool in summer; it makes me look like a sailor without the torture of seasickness.'

The same newspaper ran a special report on shaving in November 1976. Some comments that occurred:

'A beard certainly makes life easier. As a shaver I was what you might call an ear, nose and throat man, able and likely to cut anything on the head. Now the day no longer starts with blood and oaths. All I have to do is cut off the curly bits with the five-bob scissors bought for the purpose, and keep clear a hole for the eyes and nose with my son's razor.' (W L Webb)

'Shaving for me is a chore, is a bore. It's on a par with filling in income tax forms, washing the car, or listening to Mrs Thatcher talk about the underprivileged. I tried growing a beard once, in simple disgust. It took me three weeks while I was away on holiday and if I do say so myself it did look very refined. But it had to go. In the end I just felt itchy, hot, and downright unclean. But making it go was a massacre.' (Philip Jordan)

'After years of painful wet shaving and ineffective electric razors I was given a heaven-sent opportunity to grow a beard. I collapsed while crossing Threadneedle Street, carved open my chin on a traffic bollard and ended up with a lot of stiches, and some fancy scars. A few weeks in hospital gave

me the chance to establish a decent growth before having to appear in public. (The thought of several weeks of "tatty growth" had put me off the idea of growing a beard in the past.) However, beards have some disadvantages. Small children, for example, seem to be filled with an insatiable desire to see if it's false, while babies regard it as an ideal adjunct to the human climbing frame.'
(Nicholas Bannister)

That is two for and one against beards, but even though Philip Jordan felt obliged to give up his 'refined' beard, he was decidedly unenthusiastic about the return to shaving. As for Nicholas Bannister's need to hide scars, he is not the first to grow a beard for such a reason. The Emperor Hadrian, who gave his name to the wall in the North of England, is said to

John Steinbeck (1902–68) cultivated his beard 'as pure unblushing decoration'.

have worn a beard because of the same problem.

Ronnie Payne, author and journalist, once described his personal beard history as follows: 'The first beard was when I was young and foolish and a marine. A brief experiment. Then came the "intellectual" beard at Oxford: partly idleness and partly affectation. It saved me the trouble of having to shave and I rather fancied myself. Then came the job hunt and things took a turn for the ugly: beards weren't popular in newspaper offices at the end of the forties and nor were graduates. I razored it off and it stayed off until I became a foreign correspondent, when it became a Hemingway beard. I've had it ever since.'

D H Lawrence (1885–1930) believed men wore beards like neckties, for show.

BEAUTIFUL BEARDS

D H Lawrence said in 1925 that in his opinion men wore beards like neckties, for show. John Steinbeck would presumably have agreed with him. In his autobiographical *Travels With Charley*, Steinbeck comments frankly: 'I wear a beard and mustache but shave my cheeks; said beard, having a dark skunk stripe up the middle and white edges, commemorates certain relatives. I cultivate this beard not for the usual given reasons of skin trouble or pain of shaving, nor for the secret purpose of covering a weak chin, but as pure unblushing decoration, much as a peacock finds pleasure in his tail. And finally, in our time, a beard is the one thing a woman cannot do better than a man, or if she can, her success is assured only in a circus.' (Elsewhere Steinbeck remarks: 'I pulled at my beard, which is said to indicate concentration.')

Some ancient Egyptian kings used to entwine their ceremonial beards with gold threads. Indian princes, it seems, put jewels in them. In his autobiographical novel *Cider With Rosie*, Laurie Lee recounts one of his mother's vivid memories. As a girl she was working as a junior servant in a large country house when a house-party took place. Toilet facilities, for the staff at least, were primitive. Servants were

From the tomb of the Egyptian Pharaoh Tutankhamun (c.1358–c.1340 BC) in the Valley of the Kings, a ceremonial false beard entwined with gold.

Balding, but still the sexiest man in the world (US magazine People, *1989) Sean Connery winning the Oscar as Best Supporting Actor for* The Untouchables, *1987.*

supposed to use the outside privy, but it was a bitterly cold night and the young Mrs Lee decided to take a chance. She was just about to open the door of one of the lavatories in the house when it suddenly flew open. 'There, as large as life, stood an Indian prince, with a turban, and jewels in his beard.' The young servant girl was paralysed with fear, but the prince merely folded his hands, bowed low and said: 'Please, madame, to enter.' 'I felt like a queen,' Mrs Lee told her son many years later.

Another possible reason for growing a beard is hinted at in Henry Williamson's novel *The Dream of Fair Women*. The young hero is a great admirer of the writer Richard Jefferies. 'He was one of the greatest men that ever lived!' he declared. 'Look, I'll show you his portrait.' 'Is that why you wear a beard?' she enquired, looking at the photograph.

Nineteenth-century writers constantly refer to a beard as 'the distinctive male appendage'. Modern writers are more cautious. Joseph Connolly, for example, writing about beards in the *Times*, referred to them as the 'secondary sexual characteristic'. He went on to point out that they are 'associated as exclusively with the male of the species as is, well—balding, rather oddly.'

BEARDS AND BALDNESS

One possible reason for growing a beard, of course, is to compensate for natural baldness. More unusual was the case of Francis I of France, who was involved in an accident early in 1521. The king was staying at Remorantin, in the house of a nobleman, and amused himself one day by taking part in a mock battle, with snowballs as ammunition. When one of the sides was about to be overcome, someone got over-excited and threw a burning piece of wood towards the enemy. It struck the king on the head, which in turn led to his head being shaved so that the wound could be properly treated. 'Being desirous', as an 18th-century writer expressed it, 'to recover on his chin what he had lost from his head, he let his beard grow out.' His courtiers naturally followed suit,

letting their own beards grow, though it is not recorded that they shaved their heads.

Ernest Hemingway grew a bushy beard in the 1940s when he was in Cuba. He claimed that his face had become too sensitive to shave because of constant exposure to the sun, but his hair at the time was receding rapidly and becoming very thin. It is highly likely that the beard was really compensation for the loss of head hair.

Saul Bellow, in his novel *Herzog*, has the following brief discussion about the reason for growing a beard.

'Compensation for the sudden unfortunate baldness?' said Herzog.

'Fighting a depression,' said Asphalter. 'Thought a change of image might be good . . .'

Ernest Hemingway (1899–1961). American film critic Lillian Ross noted that, in later years, Hemingway's 'patriarchal-looking beard' gave him 'an air of saintliness and innocence—an air that somehow or other never seemed to be at odds with his ruggedness'.

Incidentally, Zoilus, the carping Greek critic of the fourth century who spent most of his time attacking Homer, turned the 'compensation' idea on its head. On to his own head, in fact, which he is said to have shaved. He hoped that this would make his beard grow more strongly.

The North American Review reported in 1906 that waiters in Rome had decided that in future they should be bearded. The only suggested reason for such a decision was that the clean-shaven face was a mark of servitude; beards would prove to all that the Roman waiter was his own man. The American editor's only reaction was to shudder at the thought of 'flowing beards in proximity to plates of soup'.

In his book *Beards*, Reginald Reynolds says that beards are a form of purdah for males who lack chins or have mouths that are weak or ugly. (Purdah refers to a curtain used in India to screen women from the sight of men.) Other writers comment on the need to bring something significant to an insignificant face. 'He grew a beard to make himself visible,' writes Nina Bawden tersely, in *George Beneath A Paper Moon.*

The 'beard makes a man look more interesting' theme is echoed by Sinclair Lewis, in *Gideon Planish.* He writes: 'He had a rich brown small beard, a good thick beard for a man of twenty-nine. He had grown it to give a more interesting look to a certain common-place squatness.'

Other variations on the theme: 'He was a small man,' writes Edgar Wallace, in *Thy Neighbour As Thyself*, 'painfully thin and bald; an irregular greying beard was a decoration to a face which badly needed assistance.' 'Why don't you shave?' says Professor Higgins to Nepommuck, in George Bernard Shaw's *Pygmalion*. 'I have not your imposing appearance, your chin,' says Nepommuck. 'Nobody notice me when I shave.' An Irishman called Dr Belcher argued in the late 19th century that a beard 'makes a countenance, which without it would appear weak, full of reflection, force and decision'. Those who knew the doctor only in his bearded state no doubt examined his face with renewed interest on their next meeting.

Wearing a beard has long been an outward sign of association with a particular group. In his *Book of Days*, William Hone comments that when Francis I introduced the fashion of long hair and a short beard, immediately copied by his courtiers, the 'grave elderly men' of the time made sure that they were clean-shaven. When the court fashion reverted to clean-shaven chins, the intellectuals immediately allowed their beards to grow. The broad division in western society at the beginning of the 1990s seems to be between the clean-shaven business fraternity and the intellectual/drop-out others.

The 'intellectual' aspect means that beards are part of the academic uniform in many western countries, amongst

Orthodox Jews in New York, 1947.

younger members of the faculty, at least. Isaac Asimov writes in *A Problem of Numbers*: 'He rubbed his smooth cheek — at the age of fifty he was too old for the various beard styles affected by the younger members of the department.' Asimov also implies that he no longer needs to look intellectual, having proved the point by deeds of a more significant kind.

The actor Oliver Reed has claimed that he grows his beard 'by accident, when I forget to shave'. Maybe he forgets to shave because he has also noted that 'women seem to prefer the beard'.

GOD AND NATURE

The principal argument in favour of beards — that Nature intended men to have them, and must have had a good reason for doing so — has been expressed in many ways. Here is the version of an 18th-century Frenchman, whose rather wordy eloquence survives the contemporary translation: 'Nature made nothing in vain, and the course of her wise operations is never opposed with impunity. Is it not natural to suppose that this bushy hair which she has placed on man's face must have an influence on the salubrity of the neighbouring parts that are acknowledged to be essential? Is it possible to think otherwise, without accusing our common mother of inconsequence, and charging her uniform conduct (which so fully explains its own motives) with folly and extravagance? How is it possible then for people to venture to thwart the wisdom of her intentions, and destroy their effects, without being afraid of drawing on themselves a superabundance of evils, to which human nature is already too much subject? This, however, is what we do every day, in order to comply with a very unnatural custom.'

Rather similar thinking, substituting God for Nature, leads to the beards of Orthodox

Jews. Leviticus 19, verse 27, specifically says: 'You shall not round off the hair on your temples or mar the edges of your beard.' Islamic regulations, however, recommend the trimming of the beard and moustache, though presumably for the purposes of hygiene rather than fashion.

In Europe a beard may be trimmed in order to change the shape of the face, lengthening it or making it seem more rounded. In *The Dream of Fair Women*, Henry Williamson also suggests that the beard can affect the overall impression of height: 'You're very tall; and your beard makes you appear taller.' (The same novel has a woman character who makes the far more devastating comment to a young man of twenty-two: 'You should shave it off at the earliest opportunity. I am sure you would look much nicer. It is only a pose, isn't it?' 'I hoped it was a beard,' replies the young man, lamely.)

Jerry Grange-Taylor, a bearded architect who says that he comes from a 'hairy family', began to grow his beard in his mid-forties when he contracted mumps from his small son. 'I had not shaved for ten days when my wife foresaw possibilities of great improvement in my appearance if I persevered. There followed several adjustments. First with sides removed, leaving moustache and isolated beard. Secondly the moustache went. Besides a moth-eaten appearance it had a grim effect that was not quite me. An isolated beard persisted before

it was extended to rejoin the side whiskers.'

Arthur Holden, aged 21, had this to say: 'I don't like shaving because afterwards my skin feels horrible and I come out in a rash. I'm growing a beard because it seems a practical thing for me to do now. It doesn't grow much. Perhaps I'm not manly enough? If it gets hot, sticky or itchy I'll just shave it off. It's a real waste of money buying all those shaving creams, razor blades, after-shaves. After all, what do you need except a sharp blade and cold water? And yet there's a multi-million-pound industry out there connected with shaving.'

Many young men will sympathize with that practical view. Indignant middle-aged people, of course, are likely to put your g men's beards down to laziness or a lack of personal hygienic standards which were perhaps once imposed by a spell of military service. Others see them more sympathetically as a protest not just against middle-class respectability or a particular set of conventions, but against the hypocrisy of a society that is far too concerned with outward appearance. The young men themselves simply do not care about such things. 'They are giving the world a visual lesson in priorities,' said John Sparrow, formerly Warden of All Souls' College, Oxford, in a BBC radio talk some years ago.

A rather special reason for growing a beard is mentioned by John Brophy in his book *The Human Face*. He remarks there that most kaisers, emperors and despotic kings seem to have been bearded and adds that the majesty of monarchy made it impossible for a king to shave himself; it would have had to be done by a barber. Since a despot would probably not have relished the idea of a man with an open razor having access to his throat — the temptation to do something other than shave it might prove too strong — a beard may have seemed a more prudent solution.

The English royal barber in former times was in fact a relatively important person, but subject to strict control. A 16th-century document says that 'it is also ordained that the King's barber shall daily by the King's uprising be ready and attendant in the King's Privy Chamber, there having in readiness his water basins, knives, combs, scissors and such other stuff as to his room doth appertain for trimming and dressing of the King's head and beard, and that said barber take a special regard to the pure and clean keeping of his own person and apparel, using himself always honestly in his conversations without resorting to the company of vile persons or of misguided women, in avoiding such danger as by that means he might do unto the King's most royal person'.

Also on this subject, J Cuthbert Hadden, writing in the *English Illustrated Magazine* in 1893, reports on a medieval custom of embedding three hairs of the royal beard in the wax of the seal in order to give greater solemnity to a document.

BIRDY BEARDS

Back to more ordinary mortals, and we are told that the hero of *The Exhibitionist*, by Henry Sutton, 'asserted himself with a tawny little beard that he stroked all the time. Some of the girls thought he was attractive, but most of them, Merry included, thought he looked birdy.' The author goes on to suggest a possible motive for growing a beard: 'She had never been kissed before by anyone with a beard. Perhaps that was part of the program, too, deliberately thought out, so that, if only for the sake of curiosity, the first kiss was no trouble for him.'

Beards became more common in Ireland during the early 1920s. Loyal Irishmen, whether or not they were active members of the Irish Republican Army, wore beards in order to make it more difficult for the police to identify suspects.

A more domestic reason for growing a beard may apply if a man has young children. In his novel *Love In Quiet Places*, Bernard Thompson has a young boy remark that a bearded uncle would give him some prestige at school. Perhaps a bearded father confers equal distinction.

SPECIAL PLEADING

Here are some of the zanier reasons for growing a beard. In a tract published in 1860, a writer calling himself Theologos argued that the beard was obviously meant by Nature to provide the equivalent of a

Two woodcuts from John Bulwer's Anthropo-metamorphosis.
(Left) Whiskered like the cat — a native of 'the Kingdome of Mancy in great India', 17th century.
(Right) Shaving only one side of the face — a tribal custom in Virginia in the 16th/ 17th century.

woolly scarf for the working man, 'softening the keenness of the advancing blast'. Women had not been provided with such weather protection, argued Theologos, because they were 'never intended to be exposed to the hardships and difficulties men are called upon to undergo. Woman was made a help-meet for man, and it was designed that man should, in return, protect her to the utmost of his power from those external circumstances which it is his duty boldly to encounter.'

Then there is the beard grown as a kind of pacifier, or baby's dummy. Chewing one's beard is a curious kind of cannibalism, but it is practised, it seems, by some. Ivan Ivanovitch is a character in *Dr Zhivago*, by Boris Pasternak. He is described as 'a thin, fair-haired man, restless as an eel

and with a wicked little beard which made him look like an American of Lincoln's time; he was always bunching it up in his hand and nibbling the tip'.

It is curious that mutton chops, which sound quite tasty, would not lend themselves to nibbling. They happen to be side-whiskers, shaped like mutton chops, but not within reach of the mouth.

Also connected with eating is this, from John Bulwer, writing in the 17th century about a visit to Ireland. He reported that bearded Irishmen were inclined to use their beards 'instead of napkins, to wipe their greasie fingers'. Then there was Gaspard de Coligny, Marshal of France in the 16th century, who is said to have used his beard as a kind of pin-cushion for tooth-picks.

Speaking of cushions, in

earlier times they were apparently sometimes stuffed with human hair. Beards were certainly popular amongst the Elizabethans, but only beards that were well trimmed. Seventeenth-century literature therefore contains many sarcastic references to long beards as being suitable only as stuffing. Shakespeare, in *Coriolanus*, has Menenius say to two tribunes: 'When you speak best unto the purpose, it is not worth the wagging of your beards; and your beards deserve not so honourable a grave as to stuff a botcher's cushion or to be entombed in an ass's pack-saddle.'

But does a beard act as a kind of natural cushion, a useful kind of chin guard for a boxer as a protection against an uppercut? Apparently not. John Sherwood, in his novel *The Half Hunter*, writes: 'The most infuriating thing about him was his beard, and Jim lashed out at it with all his might. To Jim's surprise, the normal amount of anguish shot through his knuckles. He had vaguely expected the beard to have an upholstering effect . . .'

Sherwood continues with a description of the fight, and lends support to Alexander the Great's theory that a beard can be a distinct disadvantage when it comes to hand-to-hand combat: 'The beard was becoming an obsession with him — it brushed against his face as they wrestled. He took a firm grip on it and pulled hard. The effect was astonishing. Jim had merely intended to commit an outrage, remembering vaguely that beard-pulling, as a

mode of inflicting deep personal humiliation, dated back to ancient times. He had no idea whether it would hurt or not. From Prentice's reaction, it evidently did . . .'

So, no joy for boxers, but beards can have other uses. *Daddy's Whiskers*, a children's story by Steve Charney, is about a father with 'wild, wild whiskers, the most incredible beard there's ever been'. The rest of the family use it as a broom, a brush to paint the living room and a shelter from a storm. The publisher's blurb says that the story offers 'a light-hearted lesson about making the most of one's resources'!

BEARDS BORNE OUT

The following, then, are 40 positive reasons that have been mentioned for growing a beard:

- a beard adds to male sex appeal
- makes a man look stronger
- makes him look more independent
- adds maturity
- adds sophistication
- adds virility
- avoids the need to cut the face to pieces with a razor
- saves money otherwise spent on razors, shaving creams, etc.
- avoids a stubbled face at the breakfast table
- avoids five o'clock shadow
- looks distinguished
- Nature intended man to be bearded
- God intended man to be bearded
- warms the face in winter and

cools it in summer
- makes a man look like a sailor without the tiresome business of having to go to sea
- covers facial scars
- makes a man look intellectual
- is decorative in its own right
- is something that the (normal) woman cannot do
- shows admiration of a role model
- compensates for baldness
- changes a man's image
- makes a dull face look interesting
- hides a weak chin or mouth
- shows group membership
- saves time and energy spent on shaving
- changes the shape of a face
- baffles the police
- demonstrates a man's attitude to the hypocritical concern for outward appearance that plagues far too many people
- arouses the curiosity of girls about what it is like to be kissed by a bewhiskered man
- makes a man look daring
- makes him look decisive
- shows that he is not servile
- confers prestige on one's child
- can provide hair to stuff a cushion
- provides something to suck
- can be used to store tooth-picks
- is useful for wiping one's hands when they get dirty
- acts as a woolly scarf
- is there as a stand-by paintbrush or broom.

By now, of course, if you are a male over the age of fifteen, you are glad you took our advice and began growing a beard when you started reading this chapter.

BOLD BEARDS

If you are still not convinced that you should have a beard, then read what follows. It comes from a book called *The Human Hair* by Alexander Rowland: 'Deprive the lion of his mane, the cock of his comb, the peacock of the emerald plumage of his tail, the ram and deer of their horns, and they not only become displeasing to the eye, but lose much of their power and vigour. The caprice of fashion alone forces the Englishman to shave off those appendages which give to the male countenance that true masculine character indicative of energy, bold daring, and decision.'

J A Dulaure, who wrote a passionate defence of the beard in 1786, at a time when all European men were clean-shaven, also mentions fashion. After 140 pages of detailed arguments, dealing with changing attitudes to beards through the centuries, he came to write his conclusions, which he did with his customary eloquence. It is worth considering his words today, at a time when the western world is once again at the end of nearly a century of general beardlessness.

'Will reason, and the constant desire of nature at length determine the men of the present day to adopt the custom of long beards? I don't believe it. The power of working such a revolution is reserved for opinion and fashion. But there are men in society who ought to be independent of those two wavering powers: these are those that govern the people, and whom religion and the state have entrusted with their interests and powers. These mediators between God and man, between the law and the citizen, who are not of the ordinary class, should be distinguished from those that are so . . .

'All the virtues which their state requires are not sufficient, they must likewise have the appearance. People see only by their eyes; it is only physical objects that have the power of captivating their veneration or exciting their contempt.

'Of all the exterior means that can attract the admiration of the people, a long beard is without doubt the most powerful, the only natural one, and which cannot be reasonably taxed with vanity or pride. Our forefathers always thought that both religion and morals were interested in the support of this ornament of man's face. And truly, what priests were ever more respected than those old white-bearded ones of the ancient religions, especially the patriarchs of the Israelites?

EFFEMINATE FACES

'If the constant seeing of objects which have the appearance of grandeur and majesty stir up the soul and give it a spring, the sight of objects which have the appearance of weakness insensibly enervate and degrade it. The man who beholds in another only the picture of effeminacy soon learns to withdraw his esteem from him, and to no longer respect him. People no longer fulfil the duties of society, nor do good for their own satisfaction, and if man's outward, effeminate appearance is not the sole cause of all these evils, it greatly contributes towards them.

'Should the example of some great men at length revive the custom of long beards, our delicateness and urbanity might again be reconciled with the majesty of man. Would it not be possible for people of good taste to give the beard an agreeable form, in the same manner as was done some centuries ago? It can never be denied: a man should appear as nature made him.'

So far, we have been concerned not so much with a defence of the beard as with an assault on those 'unnatural' men who shave, or those who speak badly of the beard. We will now allow those defendants to speak for themselves in a new chapter, though it is difficult to see how they can counter the arguments we have presented. Quite simply, a beard was obviously meant to be.

2 *Beards abandoned*

In spite of the evidence we have just produced to show that all men clearly should be bearded, we have to accept that men who wear beards in modern times are as much an oppressed minority group as the smokers. They constantly have to defend themselves. Some of the questions most often put to a man with a beard, according to Joseph Connolly in a *Times* article in 1986, are:

- Why did you grow it?
- What are you hiding?
- Have you ever thought of shaving it off?
- Does it make you hot?
  On this last point Mr Connolly pointed out that no one ever asks a person whether the hair on his head makes him hot.

An informal survey amongst male friends and colleagues reveals three main reasons why men do not grow a beard or moustache:

- because of a wish to conform, not to be thought of as an outsider in any way,
- because of a belief that a soft, clean-shaven face is more sexually attractive to women in general, or perhaps to one woman in particular,
- because shaving gives a feeling of cleanliness.

PROFESSIONAL POGONOLOGY

Where conformity is concerned, this may be something imposed from outside. In the past, bank employees and other clerks who had dealings with the public were often instructed by their employers to be respectably clean-shaven. Some modern employers still prefer to see employees with clean-shaven faces, offering a variety of reasons for their preference. An English water board, for example, according to Geoffrey Wansell in a 1983 *Times* article, said that a bearded man might frighten housewives in isolated farms, though women who are prepared to live in such places probably do not frighten easily. Firemen are told, or soon learn, that a beard can get in the way of breathing apparatus. Security men are asked to remain clean-shaven because a bearded face is more easily forged on an identity card.

Bearded policemen are seen from time to time in Britain, though at least one diligent police chief thought that a beard might make it difficult for an officer to administer the kiss of life. It is odd, though, that one of the slang names for the police is 'the fuzz', since policemen are not especially noted for their facial hair. The expression is said to have originated among black Americans in the 1930s. Policemen were usually white, and white men in general were known to the black community as fuzzy balls.

One well-known British policeman with a beard is the Chief Constable of Greater Manchester, James Anderton, the only British policeman of his rank with a beard. He has been quoted as saying that he felt a compelling need to be 'different'. He has also said that a bearded male face is 'as God and nature intended'. His Belgian colleagues would apparently not agree with him. Policemen in Ostend were

Bearded 'as God and nature intended', Chief Constable James Anderton in 1987.

recently ordered to remain clean-shaven. Local police chiefs explained that this was for their own good — criminals might set fire to their beards.

When policemen appear as witnesses in British courts, they will not see many bearded barristers, solicitors or judges. An English barrister remarked recently that in 20 years he had only ever seen one bearded judge, and one other with a moustache. The legal profession is a decidedly clean-shaven one, he said.

In 1535 in France there was an Edict of Beards which forbade anyone to appear in the halls of justice with a long beard. This applied not only to members of the legal profession, but to anyone whose affairs required him to attend the court. There are recorded cases of upright citizens of the time being refused justice until they had shaved.

Lawyers, incidentally, seem to have ruled long ago on the question of when a beard becomes a beard, rather than stubble — designer or otherwise. The English legal profession came up with a definition in the 16th century, deciding that a beard meant an unshaven facial growth of two weeks or more. Any member of Lincoln's Inn in 1550 with such a growth was not allowed to dine in the hall. This rule was later amended to allow bearded members to dine with their colleagues, though they had to pay heavily for the privilege.

When a British company was taken over by the Americans in 1985, the men who worked in its computer department were surprised to find that their new bosses forbade them to wear beards. As a *Times* journalist pointed out, this might have been called a Victorian attitude, had the later Victorians not been so strongly in favour of beards. The writer of the *Times* article went on to wonder whether the American parent company was really willing to risk a work-to-rule over the issue, 'not a go-slow so much as a go-hairy'. Or could there be a strike — or a lock-out — either of which would make the company look ridiculous?

There was also the question of the Sex Discrimination Act. If the company had insisted that all employees wear a beard, there would have been a clear case to answer, but was it not equally discriminating to introduce a contractual clause that affected men only? If employees capitulated and signed the new contracts, the *Times* writer still saw plenty of opportunity for employer harassment. An employee might not wear a beard, but there was presumably nothing to stop him wearing a long and drooping moustache, perhaps linking up with bushy side-whiskers.

Two employees at the Disneyland Hotel in Los Angeles were sacked in 1988 for refusing to shave. Mike Searles was not willing to part with his handlebar moustache, and Mike Farrington saw no reason to lose his grey-flecked beard and moustache. Some newspapers, commenting on the sackings, thought it strange that Disneyland should object to

Walt Disney (1901–66), and his bearded heroes 'off to work' in the 1937 classic, Snow White and the Seven Dwarfs.

facial hair, especially since Walt Disney himself wore a moustache. Some of the well-loved Disney characters, such as the seven dwarfs, were bearded. Commentators were also interested to note what Disneyland considered to be the female equivalent of the offending beards and moustaches, likely to spoil the clean-cut Disney image. Women employees were forbidden to wear trousers, long fingernails and heavy make-up.

Two comments on this kind of ruling from the 1960s: 'I am certainly not going to shave now.' (This was Paul S Finot, a teacher of political science at John Muir High School in Pasadena, California. In September 1963 he was removed from his teaching duties because he had grown a

beard during the summer vacation.)

'Beards, like above the knee skirts, are becoming more a fashion and less a measure of social defiance.' (Leonard Sandler, on behalf of the New York Civil Liberties Union, December 1967. The Union successfully defended the right of a transit Authority employee, Abe Dweck, to wear a beard while working.)

POLITICAL POGONOLOGY

More recently, in January 1985, it was widely reported in the British press that Margaret Thatcher had been heard to say at a party: 'I wouldn't tolerate any Minister of mine wearing a beard.' Mrs Thatcher later denied that she had ever said any such thing, but journalists had meanwhile pointed out that there were at that time 396 Tory members of parliament, only

three of whom wore beards. Three others wore moustaches. None of these six was in Mrs Thatcher's Cabinet.

On the other hand, said the journalists, Tory party chairman

Four times prime minister, and the oldest, William Ewart Gladstone (1809–98) wearing a saucer or trencher beard.

John Gummer had formerly sported both a moustache and beard. Since removing them, his career seemed to have taken off in a big way. 'Yes,' said Mr Gummer, 'I shaved to please a woman, but it was my wife, not Margaret Thatcher.' One of the bearded Tory MPs, Gregory Knight, stoutly maintained that he would not shave in response to any pressure, real or imagined.

But the fact is that in modern times, a beard is likely to make a political statement, whether the wearer intends it to do so or not. An informal survey carried out in London in 1989 revealed that most people associate a beard with someone who is at least left-wing, perhaps revolutionary. It is thought that the bearded man is also more likely to be a Green. Present-day candidates for political office, of no matter which party, are therefore usually advised to become clean-shaven. There is always the possibility that a beard will antagonize some of the voters.

This represents a great change from the end of the 19th century, when a majority of MPs were bearded. Beards then still had associations with wisdom, maturity and paternal authority. The modern view was perhaps summed up by G K Chesterton, who said of George Bernard Shaw's flowing beard: 'He's nailed the Red Flag to his face.'

It is not only in the US and Britain that a moustache or beard makes some kind of political statement in modern times. Amir Taheri reported in 1983 in a *Sunday Times* article on the situation in Turkey, where 'the sporting of beards and moustaches is taken as a possible sign of anti-regime tendencies, so they are now banned at universities and government offices. Different types of facial hair are said to symbolise different tendencies. A round thick beard is considered to be a sign of Khomeini leanings. A goatee represents a penchant for one of the many varieties of Marxism. Those wearing Errol Flynn moustaches are supposed to be Social Democrats. A thicker moustache denotes fascist opinions.'

In his book, *Garibaldi's Defence of the Roman Republic*, the historian G M Trevelyan remarks that the wearing of a beard in the early 19th century was a sign of having advanced ideas. Beards were therefore prohibited in Sicily until the 1850s. The Sardinian Consul at Trapani was forced to invoke his consular rights to save himself from being forcibly shaved by the police.

SERVICEABLE BEARDS

In the Royal Navy, sailors do not ask permission to grow a beard; they seek their captain's permission to discontinue shaving. When they want to become clean-shaven again they ask permission to recommence shaving. They are only allowed to grow a full-set, moustache with beard. The general feeling is that sailors look good in beards. Lt-Com. Buddy Barker, asked about his own beard, said he thought of it as part of naval tradition. He added that the ladies liked it.

As for the Army, arguing (in 1861) that soldiers should be allowed to wear beards in order to lighten their kit of shaving gear and save them the time spent shaving every day, Lt-Col. E Napier referred to 'what Providence has no doubt, for wise purposes of His own, planted on the face of man'. The image is a quaint one, likening the beard to a cultivated suburban garden rather than a natural landscape.

Modern warfare introduced a new problem for bearded men. Gas masks which fitted their clean-shaven colleagues could not accommodate bushy or lengthy beards. These had to be removed — they endangered the lives of those who wore them. In former times, the protective helmets worn by fighting men were sometimes specially designed to allow for a beard.

Alexander the Great would not have approved of such things. He ordered the beards of his soldiers to be removed before they went into battle, explaining that they were likely to be engaged in close fighting. He did not want their opponents to be able to grab them by their beards. This anecdote makes one think of the Abantes, an ancient war-like people who shaved the front of their heads as well as their chins. They also wanted to ensure that their enemies had nothing to grasp while they faced them in close combat. As proud warriors, however, they made a point of letting their hair grow long at the back of their necks. This was meant to show that there was no question of their being seized while running away.

BIBLICAL BEARDS

The 12th-century militant churchman Orderic Vitalis was not in favour of beards; indeed he is said to have regarded the wars and disease of his time as God's punishment for human wickedness, as represented by the wearing of long hair and beards. One of his typical declarations was: 'In former times penitents, captives and pilgrims usually went unshaved and wore long beards, as an outward mark of their penance or captivity or pilgrimage. Now almost all men wear curled hair and beards, bearing upon their faces the tokens of their filthy lust, like stinking goats.'

In the 16th century French priests, by an edict of the parliament of Toulouse, were forbidden to wear beards. Some priests managed to keep their beards because of an ambiguity in the French language, where the verb *porter* means both to wear and to carry. They interpreted the edict as a ban on carrying their beards, and had a servant walk alongside them who carried it for them.

The French clerics would have objected to the edict because they were especially proud of their beards. The bishop of Bellai, for example, who was famous for his long beard, had the habit when preaching a sermon of dividing it into the same number of sections as the topics he intended to speak about — normally two or three. Another French bishop, of Grenoble, was equally well known for his fine beard. One day, when he was at table, a servant whispered to him: 'A piece of meat has fallen on your excellency's beard.' The bishop told the servant that he should have said: 'A piece of meat has fallen on the excellency of your beard.'

But does the teaching of the Bible instruct a man to grow a beard or not? Dr John Doran refers to the Jesuit casuists, who devote themselves to thinking about matters of conscience. They have written on the matter of beards, says Dr Doran, 'and most lucidly proved, under three heads — first, that we are bound to shave the beard; second, that we are bound to let it grow; third, that we may do either the one or the other'.

The Bible may tolerate beards, but religious extremists have sometimes banned them. Two well-known examples of pogonic persecution occurred in the USA. Joshua Evans, an 18th-century Quaker who lived in New Jersey, upset his fellow Friends by his singular behaviour. He was a vegetarian, would not wear dyed fabric and objected to leather from beasts that had died violently. He also had a beard, and on this account a special committee was appointed to visit him and ask him to remove it. Joshua refused, and used many quotations from the Bible to defend his beard. He also said that many Protestant martyrs were bearded.

In spite of these valid arguments, Joshua was forbidden to travel in the ministry for some 14 years. When he was eventually liberated, as the Quakers expressed it, he wrote: 'The wearing of my beard, I believe hath been of great use in the cause I am engaged to promote; for I apprehend thousands have come to meetings, where I have been, that otherwise I should not have seen; many being induced, in great measure, to come on account of my singular appearance.'

Joshua Evans died, a much-respected man, in 1798. His Journal explains that he chose to grow a beard because he believed that only pride had caused men to shave in the first place. But he records in his book that 'great offence was taken, bitter reflections were uttered and false reports spread'. For years, in fact, many of his fellow Quakers had refused to sit next to him, though his beard had certainly not been grown for reasons of vanity. Perhaps he upset the Friends because by inference he was telling them that their clean-shaven state showed that they, not he, were the vain ones.

As for the other instance of pogonic oppression, there can be few men upon whose tombstone are the words: 'Persecuted for wearing the beard,' but such is the case with Joseph Palmer. He moved to Fitchburg, Massachusetts, in 1830, and immediately annoyed his neighbours because he wore a beard. The feeling in the community at that time was strongly anti-beards, perhaps because a powerful religious leader in the area happened to dislike them. An even stronger feeling was that all members of the community should conform to a common standard. Eccentric individuals, rebels, were not wanted. Palmer was told very firmly to remove his beard if he intended to stay in the community.

Palmer saw no reason why he should do so and refused. His behaviour, in insisting on remaining bearded, led to official and unofficial persecution. He was reprimanded in church, and eventually refused holy communion. The windows of his house were broken, children mocked him, and he was ostracized by adults. Finally he was attacked in the street by four men who forcibly tried to remove his beard.

Palmer resisted, using his pocket knife in self-defence, but was arrested for unprovoked assault. This injustice angered him greatly, and he refused to pay the fine that was imposed. He was sentenced to a year's imprisonment. While in prison Palmer continued to grow his beard. He also wrote letters about what had happened and smuggled them out to various newspapers. The citizens of Fitchburg found that the rest of the country was laughing at them. They hastily decided to drop all charges against Palmer and release him, but he refused to leave prison and forget the matter. In the end the authorities had to remove him forcibly from prison: the beard had well and truly won the day.

Palmer lived another 45 years, but never allowed anyone to forget what had happened. To the younger generation, his story must have sounded especially strange. They had grown up in a world where beards were once again fashionable. It is almost certain that the clergyman who conducted Palmer's burial service would himself have been wearing a beard.

Early Victorian discussions about whether it was right to wear a beard or not explored every avenue. A writer in the *London Methodist Quarterly Review*, presumably bearded himself, invoked theology and medical science to justify himself: 'It may surprise not a few when we say that the bronchitic affections under which ministers of the gospel so frequently labour, are often due to a violation of a hygienic law. The fact that the creator planted a beard upon the human male, thus making it a law of his physical being, indicates, in a mode not to be misunderstood, that the distinctive appendage was bestowed for the purpose of being worn. Moreover, physiologically considered, those views are corroborated by experience; for diseases of the throat have, in many instances, been traced directly to the shaving of the beard.

'Let, then, all our ministers of religion wear beards, for the Bible and nature are in favour of it; nor is the great head of the Church, Christ himself, ever seen in a painting without a beard; and it was said by the early Christian father, Tertullian, that to shave the beard is blasphemy against the face.'

MEDICAL MATTERS

These stirring words were obviously made necessary by contemporary attacks on the beard. Nor was the writer the first to use medical arguments. Dentists might like to give thought to this theory from an early physician: 'A beard preserves the teeth a long time from rotting, and strengthens the gums, an advantage which those who shave are generally deprived of, who almost all are tormented with a dreadful pain in the teeth, and lose them all before they are in any way advanced in age.'

Another early writer reports that after the Council of Trent in the 16th century, 'several ecclesiastics, being obliged to shave, were for some time after seized with a violent tooth-ache'. There is also a report of a German gentleman who was tormented with a violent pain in his teeth. He was advised to let his beard grow — did so — and his tooth-ache disappeared.

Early medical men had often claimed that a beard offered natural protection against various kinds of disease and infection and was generally beneficial, but as medical knowledge improved, counter claims were made to the effect that the average beard harboured millions of misanthropic microbes. Such claims, unfortunately, appear to have some truth in them. Frank

Richardson commented, in his usual humorously exaggerated way: 'It is no pleasing thing to feel that when one is talking to a bearded man one is in the presence of a huge invisible army which may at any moment send forth a brigade, a battalion, a sergeant or two, intent upon the invasion of oneself.'

The cause of the beard, it has to be said, was not helped by research carried out in 1907, when the controversy about unsanitary beards was at its height. A French investigator at the time walked with two men through Paris. One was bearded, the other was not. At the end of their walk, both men kissed a young lady whose lips had been treated with antiseptic. A sterilized brush was passed over her lips after each kiss. This was dipped into a sterile solution of agar-sugar which was immediately sealed. After a few days the solution from the clean-shaven man was shown to contain relatively harmless yeast germs. The solution from the bearded man 'swarmed with malignant microbes'.

There has been some more recent research by a Soviet scientist, Dr Mikhail Dmitriyev. The results, published in a popular Russian scientific magazine in 1985, indicated that facial hair traps and recycles noxious chemicals that the body is trying to get rid of through the pores of the skin. Instead of acting as an air filter, as has often been claimed for the beard, it can cause a build-up of unhealthy substances which are reinhaled, said Dmitriyev. A beard was especially dangerous, he added, for someone who smoked.

Let us turn away from such depressing information to quote some more entertaining medical anecdotes. There was Van Butchell, for example, the quack doctor who died in London in 1814. He used to ride in Hyde Park every afternoon on a little pony, wearing a large beard of 20 years' growth. It attracted much attention at a time when beards were very scarce.

The doctor's other claim to fame was that he had had his first wife's body carefully embalmed and put in a glass case, which he kept in his study. There was some logic in this madness, since he was entitled to a handsome annuity 'so long as his wife remained above ground'. After Van Butchell's death the glass case with his wife's body went to the museum of the Royal College of Surgeons.

It is also difficult to take seriously the findings of Cesare Lombroso, a 19th-century psychiatrist who investigated and classified the physical characteristics of thousands of convicted criminals. He discovered that men who committed crimes were likely to have sharp teeth, like those of rodents. They also had less beard growth than the normal male, though they tended to have bushy eyebrows and rarely go bald.

We must accept, though, that many people think that beards are unhygienic. British Rail officials certainly seemed to think so in 1976 when they ordered buffet steward Peter Cooper to shave, or to produce medical evidence that he needed to grow a beard. Such medical evidence would probably not be difficult to obtain. A number of skin conditions, ranging from sycosis to acne, are made worse by shaving, which often spreads bacteria from one hair follicle to another.

But even men who have no skin problems should sterilize their razors as well as change blades if they go in for wet shaving. They rarely do so. Electric razors should also be thoroughly cleaned and sterilized regularly. Razors, after all, come into intimate contact with the skin. A clean-shaven chin may look clean and hygienic, but the razor that helped to make it look that way may be thoroughly germ-ridden.

It seems that medical arguments for and against shaving are fairly evenly balanced. Before we leave the subject, consider the extraordinary case of the man who died of grief when his beard was shaved off. *The British Medical Journal*, in June 1987, reported an incident which occurred in India, where a patient who had a long and luxuriant beard was told that it would have to be removed to allow an operation to take place. The beard actually concealed a large goitre, or swollen thyroid gland, at the base of the man's neck. It was this that the operation was intended to remove.

The 59-year-old man at first

1951 advertisement for Rolls Razors, wet and dry.

What the well-dressed man of the nineteen-fifties will *not* be wearing

The whiskered extravagance of a century ago may seem odd to-day but it is quite understandable. For it is but in the last 25 years that Rolls Razor Ltd. have come into being — bringing a luxurious ease and comfort to shaving that only specialised study can design and precision manufacture produce.

thanks to ROLLS RAZOR LTD.

SPECIALISTS IN SHAVING TECHNIQUES

The Rolls Razor is the World's Best Safety. Its hollow ground blade is honed and stropped *in its case* and lasts for years.
43/6 (inc. Tax)

VICEROY

THE ROLLS RAZOR OF DRY SHAVERS

Needs no soap, water, blades or brush.
The VICEROY Electric UNIVERSAL Model, A.C. D.C. 90-250 volts, 119/6.
The VICEROY Electric A.C. Model, 200-250 volts, 95/-.
The VICEROY Non-Electric (hand-operated) Model, 90/-.
(All prices inc. Tax and apply in U.K. only)

ROLLS RAZOR LTD., Head Office, Works & Service, Cricklewood, London, N.W.2
Showrooms: 193, Regent Street, London, W.1. *(Callers only.)*

36

refused point-blank to have his beard cut off. He finally agreed to its removal at the insistence of the chief surgeon, but was clearly devastated by his appearance afterwards. Having looked at himself in a mirror, he is reported to have sighed and fallen silent. A few moments later he complained of a severe chest pain, then he collapsed and died. The two doctors concerned with the case, reporting it to their British colleagues as a matter of scientific interest, asked: 'How were we to know that he valued his beard so much that he'd die? Were we, or were we not, guilty of an offence?'

POGONIC PERSECUTION

Temporary circumstances can cause a general disappearance of beards. They rapidly disappeared in Cairo, for instance, after the assassination in 1981 of President Sadat. Police at the time were rounding up suspected Moslem extremists. Beards were known to be regarded as a sign of piety amongst Moslem fundamentalists, and the number of bearded Egyptian students had grown steadily since the Iranian revolution. In 1981 beards became a temporary embarrassment, likely to cause their owners to be picked up for long and painful interviews with the security forces. Even those who would have truthfully explained that their beards had been grown for reasons of individual taste rather than religious zeal found it more convenient to become clean-shaven.

But the most thorough persecution of the beard occurred in Russia in 1698, when Peter the Great decided to abolish them. Priests and serfs were allowed to keep them if they paid a beard tax. For the gentry, keeping a beard suddenly became very expensive. Every time a beard passed the city gates its owner had to pay a hundred roubles. It is not known why Peter the Great suddenly objected to beards, if indeed he did object to them. He may simply have hit upon a novel way of raising money, since most of the Russian nobles wore fine beards and were extremely proud of them. It is said that many of those who complied with the edict and shaved their beards retained their shorn glory and had it buried with them.

Reginald Reynolds, in his book *Beards*, suggested light-heartedly that Charlotte Elizabeth of Bavaria may have influenced the Czar, who was previously to be seen with both beard and moustache. In a letter to her aunt she mentioned that Peter the Great blew his nose with his fingers, and that the residue rested suspended on his moustache. It was not a very appetizing sight, said the duchess, especially at table. Reynolds wonders whether the lady dropped Peter a hint about his unpleasant habit, leaving him with a problem. Should he insist that all Russians should provide themselves with handkerchiefs, or should he insist that they shave? We know which solution he adopted, and that beards continued to be persecuted in Russia for the next 60 years.

The English writer Frank Richardson, who was so well known for his humorous assaults on beards that *Punch* magazine dubbed him Frank Whiskerson, once commented favourably on an American plan in 1906 to tax whiskers. It had been introduced by a certain Democratic Assemblyman called Cornish in the New Jersey Legislature. No doubt Richardson noticed that the bill was proposed on 1 April, which may have indicated just how serious it was, but he chose to ignore that fact and say that the idea was an excellent one which should be introduced to England at the earliest opportunity. He proposed that £20 per individual whisker would be a suitable tax rate. He also saw no reason why moustaches should be exempted. 'A walrus should not be allowed in the street until the man behind it had paid £20 to the government.'

CHANGES OF HEART

There are those individuals who choose to shave, after a period of being bearded, for their own reasons. David Crossen, an American businessman, said in a 1988 interview that he had grown a beard at the beginning of the 1970s. At the time he had needed a protective barrier between himself and the world. Since he no longer felt the need for such protection he was now clean-shaven.

Seth Fielding, an American psychiatrist who shaved his beard off in 1988, said that he had grown it in the first place 'out of boredom, rebellion and a desire to look older'. After ten years with it he was no longer bored or rebellious, and looking older seemed less of a good idea. He added, interestingly, that he was tired of people responding to his beard rather than to his face.

From a professional point of view he thought that men were likely to remove a beard once they felt confident about their sexuality. They might also want to make a fresh start socially with a new image, especially if their lives were not very satisfactory.

Robert Yesselman, general manager of the Paul Taylor Dance Company, had a beard for 12 years, then shaved it off. Getting rid of his beard was, he said, a natural conclusion to finishing two years of psychotherapy. 'It's like getting out from behind the mask with a new face. I'm getting good audience reaction.'

That last remark may well refer to comments on looking younger, a frequent reaction to a clean-shaven face that was formerly bearded, especially if the beard was tinged with grey. Removing a long-standing beard may therefore, other things being equal, be as good as a face-lift, but there are — as we shall hear later — inherent dangers in the operation.

Harry Clein, a publicity agent, has twice tried shaving off his beard, twice because the first time left him feeling depressed and drained of energy, 'just like

Samson'. He grew his beard again but shaved it off in 1988. 'This time it's okay,' he was reported as saying, 'but it's still like taking the last five dollars out of your bank account'.

Vincent de Francesco, deputy director of the Fortune Society, was more poetic after explaining a few years earlier that he had removed his beard because 'it was time to change my image around'. He exuded: 'I feel free! I feel the wind against my face! It's refreshing! It's great!'

A young Englishman named James Hyde shaved off his beard in 1988 after what he described as persistent nagging by his female colleagues. They finally offered him £100 if he would get rid of it. This gave him the idea of raising money for charity by seeking other sponsors, and in half an hour he had raised £350. The money was donated to Shelter, which helps the homeless. Mr Hyde could have donated even more to charity had he accepted an offer from his macho Australian colleagues. They offered him £400 if he would keep the beard intact. The decision to shave was no doubt influenced by female comments that without it he would immediately become far more of an eligible bachelor.

One of our own colleagues, incidentally, questioned on this subject, said: 'I've worn two beards in my time. I shaved them off because I think I look lovely anyway.' We could not think of a polite follow-up to that.

Stephen Dunn, general manager of Aramis, had his beard shaved off in 1986. He was 33 years old, and had worn the beard for 10 years. At the beginning he had wanted to look older; now he wanted to look younger. Before the operation, Mr Dunn's wife, friends and colleagues were rather interested to see what he looked like clean-shaven, most of them never having seen him that way. Mr Dunn himself was heard to comment that he was rather interested to see what he really looked like. He had forgotten. The only comment recorded after the event was that of a *Standard* journalist: 'Well, never mind, you can always grow it again.'

THE LIFTING OF THE VEIL

That last remark has a serious side to it. Around 1900, as beards went out of fashion after being the norm for at least 50 years, many men presented a clean-shaven face to the world for the first time. A writer in *Harper's Weekly* commented on the result: 'The revelations are sometimes frightful: retreating chins, blubber lips, silly mouths, brutal jaws, fat and flabby necks which had lurked unsuspected in their hairy coverts now appear and shake the beholder with surprise and consternation. "Good heaven!" he asks himself, "is that the way Jones always looked?" Jones, in the meantime, is not seriously troubled. He is pleased with the novelty of his aspect; he thinks upon the whole that it was a pity to have kept so much loveliness out of sight for so

GALLERY OF BEARDS NOT
INCLUDED ELSEWHERE

Bodkin

Old Dutch

Balbo

Needle

Forked

Square-cut

*Hammer-cut, also
called Roman T*

Parted

Hollywoodian

Rimmers

*Dundrearies, also called
Piccadilly weepers*

Goatee

Olympian, also called Patriarchal or Flowing

Medium full

Round, also called Bush

Swallow-tail

Miner's also called Tile

Anchor

Spade, also called Shenandoah

Franz Josef

Sugar-loaf

Cathedral

Ducktail

Breakwater

Mutton chops

long. He cannot resist the belief that people are admiring him. At any rate, he has that air.'

Wives like Mrs Dunn, then, who married a bearded partner without ever actually seeing him clean-shaven, might be in for a shock. A painter named Liotard, who lived in the time of George I, travelled in the East and returned with a full beard which is said to have captivated the ladies. He married one of his admirers, but soon after the wedding decided to shave off his beard. Isaac Disraeli writes:

'Directly his wife saw him, the charm of that ideal which every true woman forms of her lover was broken; for instead of a dignified manly countenance, her eyes fell upon a small pinched face,
> And such a little perking chin
> To kiss it seemed almost a sin!'

This is as nothing when one considers another case reported by the same writer. He tells us of the French king Louis VII, who was foolish enough to shave off his beard without consulting his wife, Eleanor. This simple act, according to Disraeli in his essay *Anecdotes of Fashion* (*Curiosities of Literature*), was ultimately why three million men lost their lives:

'When the fair sex were accustomed to behold their lovers with beards, the sight of a shaved chin excited feelings of horror and aversion. When Louis VII, to obey the injunctions of his bishops, cropped his hair and shaved his beard, Eleanor, his consort, found him, with this unusual appearance, very ridiculous, and soon very contemptible. She revenged herself as she thought proper, and the poor shaved king obtained a divorce. She then married the Count of Anjou, afterwards our Henry II. She had for her marriage dower the rich provinces of Poitou and Guienne; and this was the origin of those wars which for three hundred years ravaged France, and cost the French three millions of men. All of which, probably, had never occurred had Louis VII not been so rash as to crop his head and shave his beard, by which he became undignified in the eyes of our Queen Eleanor.'

Perhaps one way of avoiding such terrible consequences is to be clean-shaven for part of the year, bearded for the rest. In a *Guardian* article some years ago, Richard Boston said that for some years he had followed a system of being clean-shaven in summer, bearded in winter. One result of that was that photographs of himself in both states were lodged in the *Guardian* files. The photograph at the head of his weekly column was thus likely to show him bearded and clean-shaven at surprisingly short intervals as sub-editors chose a photograph at random. Boston went on to say that he now alternated between the bearded and clean-shaven states simply because he became bored with either his bare face or his beard. One thing that did worry him was the thought that 'a beard at the bottom and baldness at the top gives the head an upside-down look'.

FUN BEARDS AND FANCY BEARDS

There is another solution to the problem that is of stunning simplicity and which every man could adopt. It is to make use of a false beard. We tend to associate false beards in modern times with stage villains of the type seen in silent movies, usually getting their come-uppance from Charlie Chaplin or some other triumphant underdog. At various times in history, however, false beards have been worn more seriously. The ancient Egyptian pharaohs wore them as status symbols. At one time in Spain a man was likely to have a number of false beards trimmed to various styles. He would choose one to suit the particular occasion, just as a present-day male might choose one of a number of neckties. There were also *barbatoriae*, masquerades, where all the men wore false beards.

'Chin-wig' was another possible way of referring to a false beard. The word occurs in this passage from an 18th-century writer: 'Towards the middle of the 14th century, false beards came much into fashion in Spain, especially in the estates of Cortez of Catalonia. The same persons had beards of different forms and colours, and could change them as they pleased. They had different ones to wear on holidays and working-days, so that a man might have a short red beard in the morning and in the evening a long black one. Everyone changed his appearance according to his interest. These chin-wigs would soon have been as much the wear as those of the head, if the abuse which was made of them had not at length attracted the attention of government. Peter, king of Aragon, expressly forbade all his subjects to wear false beards.'

One can only guess at the manner in which the chin-wigs were misused. Did they disguise erring husbands, or were they used by the criminals of the day?

As it happens, in 1508, and again in 1513, edicts were issued in Rouen, France, forbidding men to wear false beards. The fact that the authorities felt obliged to ban them, twice in a short time, shows that they were being worn in considerable numbers.

In modern times, false beards are mainly worn by actors for professional purposes, but there seems to be no reason why men should not wear them socially. They might solve a problem for the young businessman who feels obliged to be clean-shaven and formally dressed during the day, but who would like to relax in the evening under a different persona. Perhaps this does not happen at the moment because false beards are called 'false', instead of synthetic or imitation, or some other word which is not so negative. There is a tendency to think that men who wear them are false, that they are criminals who need to disguise themselves to avoid capture.

What a difference it might make if false beards were merely 'fun-beards', worn for amusement, for a temporary change of image, much as a woman might wear a wig or change her hair style? With the right kind of marketing, a cosmetics company could soon change the image of false beards, launching a new era of male fashion. There could be a revival of the *barbatoriae*, though they would have to have a new name. No problem there. Why not be one of the first to organize a 'fancy-beard party'? Male guests with real beards could decorate them for the evening. Others could come along in fancy beards of their choice and the women could wear fancy moustaches.

As for those men, in particular professional circumstances, for whom it is difficult to be bearded, the temporary beard, worn for the occasion, is as good a compromise as any. After all, it is the appearance of the bearded face that counts, not the unimportant detail of whether the growth is natural or not.

THE ANTI-BEARD BRIGADE

Here is a summary of the reasons the anti-beard brigade has come up with to justify the mania for shaving:

- a clean-shaven face shows that a man is not trying to hide a weak mouth or chin
- it shows that he is a conformist
- women prefer a clean-shaven face (and a man naturally has to do whatever women want him to do)
- some jobs and professions ban beards
- a beard might make it too easy for someone to forge a man's photo
- someone might set fire to his beard if he had one
- a beard might make people think he was politically left-wing
- a man feels cleaner without facial hair
- he can wear a gas-mask if he has no beard
- if he gets into a fight, his opponent will not be able to grab him by the beard
- a beard would harbour microbes
- a man looks younger without a beard
- he can feel the wind on his face if he is clean-shaven
- a man does not need a beard because he is handsome enough anyway
- a beard with a bald head would make a man's face look upside-down
- a beard is no longer necessary when a man has proved his manhood in some other way

Is there really anything in the above to make a man reach for the razor?

3 Beards and ladies

Penny Perrick, writing in *The Times* in 1983, described what it was like to have a bearded husband. 'I have very much liked being on intimate terms with a beard: having one's shoulder tickled by soft whiskers rather than rasping stubble is perfectly delicious. The men on whom beards sprout seem to share a rather defiant, unselfconscious quality which is equally attractive. After all, it takes a certain amount of brio to carry on bewhiskered when after-shave is continually being promoted as the 20th century's aphrodisiac.'

In the same article, however, Penny Perrick was forced to report that her grandmother 'associated beards with loonies in battered corduroy jackets and hairy socks who ran soya bean cooperatives and believed in Esperanto, solar energy and soppy poems'.

On 11 October 1839, the future Queen Victoria noted in her diary that she had met Prince Albert, who had been invited to England for a possible royal marriage. She was much impressed with him: 'Albert really is quite charming, and so excessively handsome, such beautiful blue eyes, an exquisite nose, and such a pretty mouth with delicate mustachios and slight but very slight whiskers; a beautiful figure, broad in the shoulders and a fine waist; my heart is quite going . . .'

'Can there be anything more awful in this world than a smelly, stuffy, unaired beard?' asked Carole Dix, in an article which formed part of the *Guardian*'s Special Report on Shaving in 1976. She added: 'I do see to shave or not to shave as one of the pressing problems men have to face. Does growing facial hair express an independent, sensitive, thinking mind? Or does it show that you don't like your weak chin and need to impress others with the fact you are a male?'

Miss Dix went on to remind us that women also have to decide whether to shave or not, though in their case the decision relates to hair under the arms or on the legs.

By the end of a normal day, a beard is certainly likely to have acquired a range of smells. These will probably reflect what its owner has been eating and drinking, and more importantly, the person he was with in the restaurant. This is especially true if he has been in close contact with a woman who wears perfume. Philandering husbands who are bearded therefore have to be especially careful. They may have removed stray hairs from their jackets, and burned the little notes that might incriminate them, but a wife's keen nose can quickly gather damning evidence if they have not thought to wash the odours from their beards.

MORE PROS AND CONS

As we have already seen, women can be both favourably disposed to and violently opposed to beards and moustaches, but opposers seem to outnumber those in favour. Here are some passing comments from three Australian and two English girls:

'I don't like blond beards — there's no contrast with the colour of the skin.'
'There's nothing worse than a man doing arty things with a beard.'
'I hate it when moustache hairs grow into the nose.'
'When moustaches grow over the lip they get wet and they suck them. Disgusting.'
'A pointed beard is sinister, devilish.'
'They can tickle you in all sorts of fun places.'
'Five o'clock shadow is vile.'
'As soon as my boyfriend grew a moustache I bought him a tortoiseshell moustache comb. He won't go anywhere without it. Combs his moustache twenty times a day, even in restaurants.'
'I like those incredibly waxed English moustaches. It's very English to be well groomed.'

'Not everyone can carry off a moustache. On some men it looks ridiculous.'

'I don't mind if my boyfriend doesn't shave for a day or two,' says a young woman of our acquaintance. 'I quite like rubbing my face against his stubble if I've got an itch.'

One sour critic of men's beards — she had better remain nameless — sees them as the mark of 'the parlour bolshevik, the Chelsea artist, the minor poet and the young man whose beard is his only hope of distinction.'

'I think most men do look better, dressed for dinner,' says a woman in *Gideon Planish*, by Sinclair Lewis, 'but especially a man with a beard.'

'He kissed me warmly (oh horrid, scrubbing-brush beard) . . .' writes Nancy Mitford, in *Don't Tell Alfred*.

Some women (and men) argue that to be kissed by a man with a moustache or beard is especially enjoyable. There are those who would say that, by contrast, a kiss is enjoyed rather more by a clean-shaven man than by one with a hairy face. What is really erotic is skin-to-skin contact, which facial hair lessens. The sexiness of a moustache or beard probably derives from its simple emphasis on masculinity. The woman is left in no doubt that she is being kissed by a man rather than by another woman.

'I could not endure a husband with a beard on his face,' says Beatrice, in Shakespeare's *Much Ado About Nothing*. 'I had rather lie in the woollen.' However, she is also of the opinion that 'He that hath a beard is more than a youth, and he that hath no beard is less than a man.'

Aunt Abbie, the formidable but highly amusing character created by Dane Chandos in *Abbie*, has firm views about everything, including beards. Her opinion of the latter is expressed in a letter to her nephew: 'When I heard that I was to be decorated, I let it be known that I did not wish to be kissed on either cheek if the presenting general had a beard.'

ALL-OUT ATTACK

An outspoken article on beards that appeared in the *Chicago Chronicle* in 1903 was unusual in being written by a woman. Edith Sessions Tupper must have been a formidable personality, and she pulled no punches. She was ostensibly attacking beards, but it is difficult not to see her remarks as a more general attack on men.

'Welcome with joy,' she began, 'the tidings that a

Painter to the Court of Charles I, Sir Anthony Van Dyck, or Vandyke (1599–1641).

Charles I (1600–49) with a Vandyke.

distinguished physician has declared war on the beards of men, denouncing them as harbors of dirt and disease. If the 20th century should remove whiskers from the face of mankind, it will be glory enough for one hundred years.'

Edith Tupper went on to anticipate the modern approach to such subjects by interpreting different types of beard. There was what she called 'opinionated whiskers', often seen on clergymen. These whiskers, long and narrow, announced to the world: 'I am it.' Opinionated whiskers is rather a subjective description, but Miss Tupper then turned to the Van Dyke, about which there could be no argument. 'I never saw a man wearing a Van Dyke beard who was not selfish, sinister and pompous as a peacock. Many men consider this beard artistic. I believe

artists do affect it. The man with the pointed beard takes himself very seriously.'

Back to subjective description, and what the writer thought were 'unctuous whiskers — the whiskers of the Mormon elder. They usually fringe full, sensual, smug, hypocritical lips. Never trust such whiskers.' Scholarly whiskers, or close-clipped sideburns, came in for slightly less abuse, being 'not so repulsive as chin whiskers'. Respectable bank president whiskers, also worn by statesmen and some clergymen, were merely dull. Back to virulent scorn for the unkempt, matted whiskers of the anarchist, 'a ferocious setting for the savage face'. As for the whiskers of the rural districts, they reminded Miss Tupper of the cornstalks and haystacks which were also to be seen there.

A back-handed compliment for moustaches followed all this. 'If a man must wear hair on his face, let it be in this shape.' Mustachioed readers probably breathed a sigh of relief at this point, but Miss Tupper had not yet finished. 'A mustache often covers ugly teeth and lips, thereby proving a boon to mankind.'

Miss Tupper summed it all up as follows: 'There is a certain distinction about the clean-shaven man which the wearer of whiskers can never possess. Moreover, a smooth face is a stimulant to high thoughts. For behind walls and hedges and brambles of hair mean, low, cunning thoughts can conceal their traces, but they are blazoned forth on the open of a smooth cheek.'

BEARDS REMEMBERED

Recalling her experiences as a secretary in the 1930s, Agnes Kinnersley described in an *Accountancy Age* article in 1988 the Bearded Terror for whom she once worked. He was actually the senior partner in a firm of chartered accountants, and since beards were very rare at the time in that profession, his employees indulged in much speculation about the reason for the beard. 'Was it to hide the evidence of some obscure disease or the place where a well-merited punch on the jaw had left its mark? The office boy thought he had had a lucky escape from "being done" by Sweeney Todd, the demon barber of Fleet Street.' Miss Kinnersley says that newcomers to the firm thought the Bearded Terror a benign old gentleman, but soon discovered he was a tyrant.

We are not sure whether the following is in favour of, or against the idea of face fungus. Mrs Katy Clarke writes to say: 'When I first met my husband I could not hide the fact from my parents that we'd been "snogging". Having both beard and moustache meant that Peter marked me as his own, for I had a red friction mark shining like a beacon for attention on my upper lip. I looked like a kid with jam round my mouth! Now 13 years into marriage with Peter I no longer have this problem. Either I have become

immune or the mad fervour is more evenly spaced.'

A bearded or bewhiskered man, for some women, is a suspicious character. George Orwell, in his *Down and Out in Paris and London*, describes a young Italian who arrived one day at the hotel where he was staying. 'He was rather an ambiguous person, for he wore side whiskers, which are the mark either of an apache or an intellectual.' By 'apache' Orwell meant ruffian, that term being used to describe a street robber in Paris. Orwell's landlady was decidedly suspicious and made her side-whiskered guest pay a week's rent in advance. He duly stayed six nights, during which time he managed to obtain duplicate keys to various rooms. Orwell's room was one of those which he robbed before he left.

A quiet little put-down of a self-satisfied bearded male occurs in *Moses*, by Susan Barrett: ' "It's a gem," said Paul. "Don't you agree? Feel it. Silky-soft with new improved Dandrufene." He took an ivory comb out of his breast pocket and ran it through his small, goatee-shaped beard. "It suits you," said Jo. "Definitely in character." "Yes," said Val, "all the smart young men about town wear shaving brushes today." '

THE BEARDED LADY QUESTION

Janice Deveree of Kentucky had a beard which was 36 cm *14 in* long when it was measured in 1842. There are reports of bearded ladies with far longer beards, but evidence that they were genuine is impossible to obtain.

Why do men have a natural growth of facial hair, while women, normally, do not? One theory is that in the distant past, women stayed in the caves to suckle the children while the men went out to hunt. The men needed facial hair as a protection against the weather; the women led more protected lives and needed only to emerge in summer. After many centuries of such differing lifestyles, women no longer produced facial hair.

The problem with this theory, taken to its logical conclusion, is that women would presumably not have needed any hair at all. By rights, therefore, all modern women should be bald.

An alternative answer to the question: why don't women have beards? was provided by an 18th-century wit. Nature arranged things that way, he announced, because it would have been impossible for a woman to shave. She would have been unable to stop talking long enough.

We think of a bearded woman as a freak. Women are simply not meant to have beards. On the other hand, men are. One philopogonist therefore made the point that a man without a beard should be considered as unnatural and ridiculous as a bearded woman.

It was at one time a common belief that an old woman with hairs on her chin was a witch. There are references to this in the Shakespeare plays. In *Macbeth*, for example, Banquo

Mademoiselle Eva, a bearded lady, 1880.

says to the weird sisters: 'You should be women, and yet your beards forbid me to interpret that you are so.'

In *The Merry Wives of Windsor*, when Sir John Falstaff is trying to escape from Ford's house disguised as a woman, Ford cries out: 'Hang her, witch!' Sir

Hugh Evans comments: 'I think the 'oman is a witch indeed. I like not when a 'oman has a great peard. I spy a great peard under her muffler!'

Women with troublesome husbands (i.e. every married woman) used to invoke the help of St Uncumber, as she was known in England. Elsewhere she was known as St Wilgefortis, or Liberata, or Livrade. According to legend, this young lady was a daughter of the King of Portugal, who wanted her to marry the King of Sicily. She had taken a vow of virginity, and prayed for help in this difficult situation. Her prayers were answered when a beard grew upon her face, causing the King of Sicily to withdraw his suit. Her father was not pleased about what had happened and had his daughter crucified. Artists represented this fictional event, showing a bearded woman hanging from a cross.

It is thought that the legend arose because of representations of Christ on the cross wearing a long tunic. The latter caused people to think that it was a woman who was being put to death.

Rabbi Lionel Blue recounts in his book *Bolts From the Blue* the question posed to him when he was a student. He was asked to imagine that he was at a Jewish wedding, where it is an obligatory custom for the guests to tell the bridegroom that he has a lovely bride. What would he as a guest do if he discovered that the bride had a beard?

One answer to this is that the woman concerned might look odd in the eyes of ordinary men, but God (for all we know) might find her perfectly acceptable. It would therefore be all right to congratulate the bridegroom. It becomes more complex if you happen to know that the bride is not only bearded, but a harlot. She is morally as well as physically ugly. What do you do in such circumstances — tell the truth or a white lie? Those interested in such questions should consult Rabbi Blue's book. He has much to say of interest on this and many other subjects.

In August 1989, various newspapers carried a report about an American teacher, Carolyn Turner, who had rather a unique way of spending her summer vacation. She disguised herself as a man, complete with false beard, and robbed five banks. Apparently the beard did not fool her victims, since the voice that emerged from behind it, telling them to hand over the cash, was clearly that of a woman. Journalists tended to treat the story as a joke ('Police pounce on a bearded lady' said the London *Times*), but the robberies were serious enough.

We leave the final comment on beards and ladies to the famous 18th-century writer and wit Voltaire (François Marie Arouet). He was often in trouble for his outspoken comments. Twice they caused him to be thrown into the Bastille. Our women readers might say that he deserved to be permanently imprisoned there. It was he who said: 'Ideas are like beards — children and women never have them.'

4 *Shavers young and old*

'A woman,' wrote the poet Robert Southey, in an article published in 1849, stands in need of one thing only, which is a good husband; but a man hath to provide himself with two things, a good wife and a good razor, and it is more dificult to find the latter than the former.'

This comment was presumably meant to be a back-handed compliment to women, though today's feminists would certainly object to the assumption (by a male, of course) that all they need is a good husband. But let us allow the comment to take us from the views of women on beards and moustaches to another topic — shaving.

CHOICES

If we consider for a moment the decision that the average man has to make about how he presents himself to the world, we see that he has many choices.

- He can allow his beard, side-whiskers and moustache to grow unchecked, reaching whatever length nature dictates.
- He can wear a beard and moustache, both of which are trimmed or shaped.
- He can wear a moustache only, choosing its particular form.
- He can wear a beard only, trimming or shaping it to a greater or lesser extent.
- He can wear full side-whiskers, while shaving the chin and upper lip.
- He can wear side-whiskers which merge into a full moustache.
- He can be clean-shaven, but with deep sideboards.
- He can be clean-shaven, with no sideboards.

There are probably other combinations, and all of these options remain open to him even when be becomes bald. Many men, in fact, compensate for baldness by making more use of facial hair. While the hair on the head diminishes, the bristles on the chin increase. Those bristles that the average man removes from his chin every day are not very long, but if they were laid end to end . . .

A German scientist once calculated that a normal man shaves off 8 m 27 ft of stubble during his lifetime. By 'normal' he presumably meant 'German', or 'European' at least. Research has shown that the facial follicles — holes in which hairs grow through the skin — of an Oriental man are eight to ten times fewer than those of the average European male. There may be less of it, but the Oriental beard, when it grows, is especially bristly.

Some men are not 'normal' when it comes to the growth of facial hair. In a remark which was presumably meant to console those who, for one reason or another, could not successfully grow a beard, F B Shuldham, MD, wrote in a 19th-century tract: 'The beard is an accident of sex, nay it is an accident of individual capacity for hair growing, but (and here comes the consolation) nature has been generous enough to give all her children a nose.' It is difficult to know what to say to that.

For the moment let us stick with those men who have more than just a nose on their face and ask ourselves why our male ancestors started to shave in the first place. It is, after all, a strange thing to do. Nature clearly intends that men and women should be distinguished as bearded and non-bearded, so shaving could be seen as a denial of natural gender, a kind of self-imposed emasculation.

Cleanliness is often advanced as a reason for shaving. It makes it possible to eat and drink without trapping debris in the hair round the mouth, but at tribal level, manliness would always have been more important than cleanliness. In some societies, shaving may once have shown that a man was wealthy enough to have time to attend to his toilet, as opposed to those who were obliged to toil from dawn to dusk. Such status symbols have always been necessary. In other cases, shaving may have been a way of distinguishing the members of one tribe from another, also very necessary when tribal warfare was commonplace.

In modern societies such distinguishing is still practised, though it now tends to be between sub-sections of the same society rather than different tribes. Present-day conformity demands clean-shaven male faces. Non-conformists, or those who wish to be thought of as non-conformists, therefore have an easy way of displaying their originality.

All that is at the general level. Individual psychological factors then come into play, determining what kind of beard or moustache a man grows, and when he grows it. Desmond Morris, some of whose theories have just been summarized, has suggested that shaving was originally, in primitive man, an 'appeasement display', a signal to others that the man concerned meant no harm to others. Removal of the beard was a deliberate reduction in the level of the man's masculinity. This should not be taken to mean that a clean-shaven man in modern times is less aggressive than a bearded man. Many would argue that exactly the opposite is true.

For some men, as we have seen, it is the horrors of shaving that justify growing a beard.

Many men, however, grow a beard or moustache and continue to shave parts of their faces. In this chapter we present a miscellany of thoughts, comments and anecdotes about shaving and clean-shaven faces.

THE BARBERS

The safety razor blade was invented by the American King Camp Gillette in 1895, and had within a few years a dramatic effect. Before the safety razor came into general use it was more common for a man to be shaved by a barber (the word derives from the French word *barbe*, meaning 'beard') than attempt to use a cut-throat razor on himself. One 19th-century beard-lover was therefore moved to attack the barbering fraternity as follows: 'As for barbers, they have always been gossips and mischief-makers. Who can respect a man whose sole office is to deprive his sex of their distinctive feature?'

The Anglo-Canadian humorist Stephen Leacock accepted the gossip notion but was more kindly disposed towards barbers. He wrote an amusing piece in 1910 called *Men Who Have Shaved Me*. His theme was that men went to a

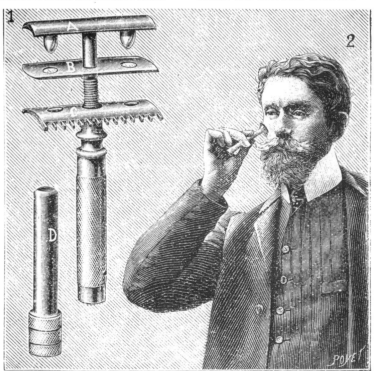

King Camp Gillette filed the patent for his invention in 1901 — within five years he had sold 90 000 safety razors and more than 12 million blades.

barber's shop to be shaved, not so much for the shave itself as for the information the barber was able to impart — especially about the sporting events of the moment. 'Every reasonable businessman is willing to sit and wait half an hour for a shave which he could give himself in three minutes because he knows that if he goes into town without understanding exactly why Chicago lost two games straight he will appear an ignoramus.'

And what of the early barbers? Pliny the Elder, in his *Historia Naturalis*, tell us: 'The first barbers that entered Italy came out of Sicily and it was in the 454th year after the foundation of Rome . . . The first that was shaven every day was Scipio Africanus, and after him cometh Augustus the Emperor, who evermore used the razor.'

Auguste Piccard, a well-known Swiss physicist who made balloon ascents into the stratosphere in the 1930s to investigate cosmic rays, is remembered also for a practical joke he once played on a barber. Staying overnight in a town where he was not known, he went into the barber's shop next morning and asked for a shave. 'Make sure it's a close one,' he told the barber. 'My beard grows so rapidly that I need to shave every two hours.' The barber rose to this professional challenge and shaved Auguste very carefully. 'You certainly won't need to shave again in two hours,' he told him, 'but if you do, I'll shave you for nothing.'

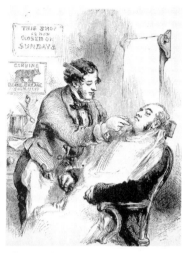

The British barber at work, 1855.

Almost exactly two hours later the barber was amazed when his customer returned with a dark stubble on his chin. 'Now do you believe me?' he asked, as he sat down for his free shave. It is to be hoped that before the barber had subsequently bored too many of his customers with the tale of the fastest-growing beard in the West, someone had mentioned to him that Auguste Piccard was not alone on his overnight visit to the town. His identical twin brother Jean Felix happened to be with him.

Axel Munthe, in his *Story of San Michele*, relates that the best shave he ever had was while making a railway journey in Germany, by a man who claimed to have shaved hundreds of men and never heard a word of complaint. After the shave he complimented the barber, and remarked that travelling was a great education as usually he was shaved while sitting in a chair but in Germany barbers preferred their clients to lie flat on their backs. The barber remarked that the custom was peculiar to him. His real job was to accompany corpses which were being sent from one place to another. He normally shaved only those who were dead and it was difficult to make them sit up.

'I could never discover more than two reasons for shaving,' says the barber in Henry Fielding's 18th-century novel *Tom Jones*; 'the one is to get a beard, the other is to get rid of one.'

CHRISTIAN CONTROVERSY

The titles of two tracts published in 1847 and 1860 respectively contain, as was so often the case with long-winded Victorian titles, a summary of everything the authors wanted to say. The first was called: 'Beard Shaving and the Common Use of the Razor; an Unnatural, Irrational, Unmanly, Ungodly, and Fatal Fashion Among Christians'. The second was called: 'Shaving — a Break of the Sabbath and a Hindrance to the Spread of the Gospel'. Neither author, needless to say, was clean-shaven.

Incidentally, husbands who do not bother to shave on Sundays can (perhaps) bring to their defence the strict observers of the Sabbath in Scotland, who said that men should not shave on that day. Lord Byron commented, in his *English Bards and Scotch Reviewers*:

Raise not your scythe,
   suppressors of our vice!
Reforming saints, too
   delicately nice!
By whose decrees, our sinful
   souls to save,
No Sunday tankards foam, no
   barbers shave,
And beer undrawn and
   beards unmown display
Your holy reverence for the
   Sabbath day.

Whatever those 19th-century Scottish moralists might have thought of it, the fact is that most clergymen today probably do shave on Sundays, as they do on every other day. It has been suggested that this is because priests have to be open in every aspect of their lives. A beard might conceal facial expression, and it is not thought suitable for a priest to conceal his true feelings. Franciscan monks and missionaries are exceptions to this rule, their beards traditionally signifying that they have returned from living amongst 'barbarians'. (This tradition is based upon the common, but false, assumption that the word barbarian derives from the Latin word *barba*, meaning 'beard'. It is in fact based on a word which means 'stammerer'. This is how the ancient Greeks described any foreigner who did not speak Greek. The name Barbara derives from the same root as barbarian, and therefore means something like 'non-Greek-speaking foreigner', not 'bearded lady'.)

In early times, too, a clean-shaven face was associated with Christianity: beards were for the

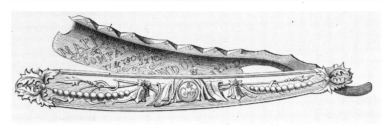

A 19th-century advertisement for a finely decorated 'cut-throat' razor by English silversmiths, Mappin & Co.

Moslem or the Jew, or the pagans of northern Europe. On Christmas Day, 1105, it is recorded that bishop Godfrey refused communion to any man wearing a beard.

The following comments set out to prove that there are moral benefits to be obtained in the act of shaving itself. They were recorded in the mid-19th century, when the cut-throat razor was universally used, and derive from the poet Robert Southey. He was talking especially of what he called the 'autokurkus', or 'self-shaver', as opposed to the man who was shaved by a barber:

'The operation brings the patient into a frame of mind favourable to his moral improvement. He must be quiet and composed: in whatever temper or state of feeling he may stand at the looking-glass, he must at once become calm. There must be no haste, no impatience, no irritability; so surely as he gives way to either, he will smart for it. And however prone to wander his thoughts may be, at other and perhaps more serious times, he must be as attentive to what he

is about in the act of shaving, as if he were working a problem in mathematics. As a lion's heart and a woman's hand are among the requisites for a surgeon, so are they for the shaver. He must have a steady hand, and a mind steadied for the occasion; a hand confident in its skill, and a mind assured that the hand is competent to the service upon which it is ordered. Fear brings with it its immediate punishment as surely as in a field of battle; if he but think of cutting himself, cut himself he will.'

THE EFFEMINATE CONTROVERSY

The essayist Leigh Hunt, also writing in the days of cut-throat razors and houses without central heating in the 19th century, had this to say in his *Getting Up On Cold Mornings*: 'I now cannot help thinking a good deal — who can? — upon the unnecessary and villainous custom of shaving: it is a thing so unmanly, so effeminate. No wonder that the Queen of France took part with the rebels against the degenerate king, her husband, who first affronted her smooth visage with a face like her own. The Emperor Julian never showed the luxuriancy of his genius to better advantage than in reviving the flowing beard. Look at Cardinal Bembo's picture — at Michelangelo's — at Titian's — at Shakespeare's — at Fletcher's — at Spenser's — at Chaucer's — at Alfred's — at Plato's — I could name a man for every tick of my watch. Look at the Turks, a grave and otiose people. Lastly, think of the razor itself — how totally opposed to every sensation of bed — how cold, how edgy, how hard! how utterly different from anything like the warm and circulating amplitude, which "Sweetly recommends itself unto our gentle senses".

'Add to this, benumbed fingers, which may help you to cut yourself, a quivering body, a frozen towel, and a ewer full of ice . . .'

Others have taken up the theme of the effeminacy of shaving. The French philosopher Rousseau, commenting on the clean-shaven faces of men which made them seem feminine, remarked: 'A perfect man and a perfect woman should be more alike in mind than in face: these silly imitations of sex are the height of folly; they make the wise man laugh and the lover run away . . . In short, I take it that, unless one be five feet six inches high, have a firm, tenor voice, and a beard on his chin, he should not pretend to be a man.'

Another 18th-century French writer, lamenting that he was living in a clean-shaven age, had this to say: 'It is a disgrace to man to have the most conspicuous mark of his virility taken off: to pretend that it becomes him to look like a woman, an eunuch, or a child, is the height of folly and ridiculousness. Even if this truth were not constantly supported by the will of nature, the opinions of all the most respectable characters of antiquity should be sufficient to establish it for ever among all nations.

'A shaved chin was always the sign of slavery, infamy or debauchery. Diogenes asked those he saw without beards, if they had not changed their sex, and were dissatisfied at being men. The loss of the beard, among a great many nations, was always accompanied by banishment. All the fathers of the church exclaimed against this shameful abuse, and always regarded a shaved chin as the effect of the vilest licentiousness.'

Clean-shaven men not only look like women, they are ruled by them said this same commentator: 'Those who bestow most attention to shaving are the most subject to petticoat government.' (J A Dulaure, in his *Pogonologia*, 1786.)

Stephen Leacock would seemingly have agreed with such sentiments. He writes in his *Further Foolishness of 'The Snoopopaths'*: 'The up-to-date, clean-shaven snoopopathic man . . . How one would enjoy seeing a man — a real one with Nevada whiskers and long

Geoffrey Chaucer (1345?–1400) with a forked beard.

boots — land him a solid kick from behind.'

As usual, there is a different point of view. Martin Luther, the leader of the German Protestant Reformation in the 16th century, would not have been moved by these 'effeminate' arguments. He is said to have believed that there was an intimate connection between shaving and sin, that the beard was ingrained in man like evil itself. Neither can be eradicated, but both must be resisted and unceasingly cut down.

Victor Kiam is the man who tells us on television that he was so pleased with the Remington shaver that he bought the company. It might be that if anyone was going to be a misopogonist, or hater of beards, it would be Mr Kiam. He has been quoted, however, as saying that he has no objection to beards. He added: 'If a man has something to hide he should certainly grow one.'

An article in the *New York Times Magazine* in the late 1960s said: 'Fortunately for Schick, Remington, Gillette and company, beards today are very much out of fashion, worn for the most part only by beatniks, aging philosophers, freelance magazine writers and Mitch Miller. Once thought of as a sign of the virile male, beards in general are now considered a sign of the chinless conformist—which is exactly the way that everyone inside the shaving industry would like everyone outside the shaving industry to keep on thinking.' The writer of this article, Edward T Ewen, seems to have been the first to apply the phrase 'lunatic fringe' to the beard itself, rather than to people with unconventional and unpopular ideas.

A general return to beard-growing could have a dramatic effect on companies producing

Remington Rand advertisement, 1937.

razors, shaving soaps and the like. In Britain alone men spend over £50 million a year on razors and blades, plus a further £20 million a year on shaving creams and foams. In 1986 14 million Britons were still using hot water, soap and razor blades to shave. Another 12 million or so were using electric razors.

One of the more successful phrases dreamed up by an advertising agent in modern times is 'five o'clock shadow'. Its success lies in its identification of something immediately recognizable, for which no term previously existed. Until the 1930s, when the phrase first appeared in American advertisements for Gem razors and blades, it was necessary to talk about something like 'the darkness on the lower part of a man's face caused by hair growing during the day after being closely shaved off in the morning'.

One who suffers from five o'clock shadow is F B White's commuter. His definition of the male commuting animal has become well known since its first appearance in 1929. It's no mean achievement to conjure up in just a few lines an image of countless clean-shaven chins packed together in the railway compartment:

> Commuter — one who spends his life
> In riding to and from his wife
> A man who shaves and takes a train,
> And then rides back to shave again.

ODDS AND ENDS

'If I had to ban anything in life, I'd ban shaving. I'm annoyed by the sheer time it takes.' This statement by the British politician and novelist Jeffrey Archer in 1986 prompted some thoughts by Joseph Connolly in *The Times*. The first thought was that if Mr Archer disliked shaving so much, why didn't he just stop doing it? Connolly was unable to answer the question satisfactorily, but hinted that Mr Archer no doubt wished to look 'normal', which was to say, clean-shaven. That is really only normal for women, Joseph Connolly went on. It only seems normal for men because, as Jeffrey Archer had complained, they spend so much time shaving. Connolly estimated this wasted time as up to 10 minutes a day, or 60 hours a year, or one and a half working weeks a year.

Ernest Boyd, writing in the *New Statesman and Nation* (August 1935), said that a bearded man in America enjoyed all the privileges of a bearded woman in a circus. He added that America was at that time the most clean-shaven country in the world.

Someone once pointed out, not too seriously, that by looking at a garden you can tell whether the gardener is clean-shaven or bearded. The clean-shaven gardener, so the theory goes, will have closely cropped lawns, and flower beds with well-defined edges. A bearded gardener will prefer something approaching a wilderness, with shrubs allowed to proliferate.

The implication is that a man who shaves prefers to order nature, while a man who allows his beard to grow would really like to be a wild man of the woods.

YOUNG SHAVERS

The first shaving of a young Roman was done with great ceremony. As an early writer expressed it: 'The first fruits of the chin were carefully collected in a gold or silver box, in order afterwards to be presented to some god, as a tribute to youth. This pious offering was mostly made to Jupiter Capitolinus.'

On the subject of young men who have not yet had reason to shave, William Thackeray writes, in *The Age of Wisdom*:

Ho, pretty page, with the
   dimpled chin
That never has known the
   barber's shear
All your wish is woman to
   win,
That's the way that boys
   begin,
Wait till you come to Forty
   Year.

Samuel Hoffenstein, by the way, has brilliantly summed up life as follows:

Babies haven't any hair;
Old men's heads are just as
   bare;
Between the cradle and the
   grave
Lies a haircut and a shave.

It used to be quite common to hear a young boy being addressed as 'you young shaver'. (Examples occur in Dickens's *Oliver Twist* and George Eliot's *Scenes of Clerical Life*.) The curious thing was that the boy concerned was nearly always too young to be a shaver in the literal sense. The expression alluded to a special sense of 'shave', which was to fleece someone of his money, to steal from him. (It is said of Henry VII, father of the bearded Henry VIII, that he 'shaved himself and fleeced his people'.) The word 'nipper', applied to a child, had a similar original meaning, someone who nipped things, stole them.

Well, it is time to turn to something new. At one stage we were thinking of throwing into this chapter a ghastly pun or two, but we decided against it. Mind you, it was a close shave. A couple of young blades like us could have made all sorts of quips, but we did not want to get you into a lather.

Henry VIII (1491–1547) from a painting by Holbein.

62

5 Bygone beards

St Gregory of Tours records the stirring tale of a Saxon army who suffered a crushing defeat at the hands of their enemies. The survivors gritted their teeth and vowed never to cut their hair or shave their beards again until they had avenged themselves.

In due time the survivors of the former battle, looking rather shaggier than before, fought again. It would be pleasant to report that they had their revenge. Not so, says St Gregory. This time they were totally wiped out.

THE BEARDLESS CULTURES

In a BBC radio talk some years ago, John Sparrow, retired Warden of All Souls' College, Oxford, described the 'two great beardless western cultures'. One was at the beginning of the Christian era, during the late Roman republic and early Roman Empire, when clean-shaven Romans were the guardians of western civilization against the bearded barbarians, the shaggy savages, who surrounded them on all sides. (Although 'barbarian' does not derive from the Latin word *barba*, 'beard', John Sparrow

thought that Roman children could hardly be blamed if they assumed that the *barbarae*, 'barbarians', were the *barbati*, 'bearded ones'.)

With the fall of the Roman Empire, the beard came into its own, prevailing for a thousand years until the end of the 17th century. There was then another generally clean-shaven period until about 1840. Steele and Addison, Jonathan Swift, Laurence Sterne, Dr Johnson, the Elder and the Younger Pitt, Crabbe, Sir Walter Scott and most other well-known men of the time were beardless. The Romantic poets, Byron, Keats, Shelley, Coleridge, Wordsworth, remained beardless, though they revolted against convention and advocated a return to nature. Even William Blake, a rebel against customs and conventions in almost every aspect of his life, was a conformist in that he remained clean-shaven.

There have been occasional attempts, nevertheless, to prove that most of the great men in history were bearded. Socrates, Muhammad, Moses, Christ, Chaucer, Shakespeare, Sir Francis Drake, Abraham Lincoln, Henry VIII, are among

William Shakespeare (1564–1616) wearing a pique-devant.

the names that are cited in evidence. The list could certainly be extended very considerably, but it would only be as useful as the similar catalogues of great men who were left-handed, homosexual, pipe-smokers, or sharers of some other habit or physical characteristic. It might provide, in other words, a beard-wearer who was feeling under siege with a little conversational ammunition, but the present-day anti-beard brigade would be little impressed.

ANTIQUE BEARDS

Dulaure, writing at the end of the 18th century, says: 'The most celebrated ancient writers, and several modern ones, have spoken honourably of the finest beards of antiquity. Homer speaks highly of the white beard of Nestor and that of old King Priam. Virgil describes Mezentius's to us, which was so thick and long as to cover all his breast; Chrysippus praises the noble beard of Timothy, a famous player on the flute. Pliny the Younger tells us of the white beard of Euphrates, a Syrian philosopher, and he takes pleasure in relating the respect mixed with fear with which it inspired the people.

'Plutarch speaks of the long white beard of an old Laconian who, being asked why he let it grow so, replied: " 'Tis that, seeing continually my white beard, I may do nothing unworthy of its whiteness." But Perseus seems to outdo all these authors: this poet was so convinced that a beard was the symbol of wisdom that he thought he could not bestow a greater encomium on the divine Socrates than by calling him the bearded master, *Magistrum barbatum*.'

William of Tyre tells a story which is meant to illustrate the former importance of a beard to a nobleman. The story appeals to us because we have not

Assyrian king, Ashurnasirpal II with a beard of spiral curls about 875 BC.

heard of anyone else pawning his beard.

Baldwin, count of Edesse, badly needed money. His father-in-law, Gabriel, was a very rich man, but it was difficult to get him to part with any of his wealth. Baldwin eventually went to him and told him that he had been forced to borrow a large sum of money. Against the loan he had pledged his beard.

'The astonishment of the father-in-law,' writes William, 'was so great at what he heard that he made him repeat the terms of this strange agreement several times. Being at length too well convinced of his son-in-law's inability to raise the cash, the credulous Gabriel bewailed his misfortune, saying: "How is it possible for a man to find in his heart to pledge a thing that should be so carefully preserved, a thing that is the proof of virility, wherein consists the principal authority of man, and is the ornament of his face. How could you possibly consider as a thing of little value what cannot be taken from a man without loading him with shame?"

'The count replied to these reproaches that, having nothing in the world that he valued so much, he had thought it his duty to pledge it to satisfy his creditors, and that he was determined to fulfil his promise if he could not immediately find the money he needed. The father-in-law, alarmed for the beard of Baldwin, instantly gave him the amount he needed, recommending him at the same time never more to pledge a property on which the honour of a knight depended.'

Harrison's *Description of England* (1586) includes comments on hair and beard styles and makes some points which are valid today. He writes: 'our varietie of beards, of which some are shaven from the chin like those of Turks, not a few cut short like to the beard of marques Otto, some round like a rubbing brush, others with a *pique devant* (O fine fashion!), or now and then suffered to grow long, the barbers being growen so cunning in this behalfe as the tailors.

'And therefore if a man have a lean and streight face, a marques Otto cut will make it broad and large; if it be platter like, a long slender beard will make it seeme the narrower; if he be wesell becked [i.e. with a weasel-beak], then much heare left on the cheeks will make the owner looke big like a bowdled hen, and so grim as a goose.' ('Bowdled' means with the feathers ruffled or swelled out, and Harrison seems to have been the only person to have recorded the word.)

His comparison of barbers and tailors is interesting. It is accepted that a good tailor should do what he can to correct the natural imperfections of a man's shape. It seems as logical that a barber should do the same with his face, by trimming a man's beard to soften any irregularities.

The Puritans of the late 16th century were disgusted by the

attention their contemporaries gave to their appearance, including their beards. One such Puritan was Philip Stubbes, who published his *Anatomy of Abuses* in 1583. He attacked the barbers of his day, at least one of whom had obviously annoyed him with his full sales patter.

The barbers, said Stubbes, 'have invented such strange fashions and monstrous manner of cuttings, trimmings, shavings and washings, that you would wonder to see. They have one manner of cut called the French cut, another the Spanish cut, one called the Dutch cut, another the Italian, one the newe cut, another the old, one of the bravado fashion, another of the meane fashion. One a gentleman's cut, another the common cut, one cut of the court, another of the country, with infinite the like varieties, which I overpasse.

'They have also other kinds of cut innumerable; and therefore when you come to be trimmed, they will aske you whether you will be cut to looke terrible to your enemie, or amiable to your friend, grim and stern in countenance, or plesant and demure (for they have divers kinds of cuts for all these purposes, or else they lie). Then when they have done all their feats, it is a world to consider how the mowchatowes [moustaches] must be preserved and laid out, and from one cheke to another, yea, almost from one eare to another, and turned up like two hornes towards the forehead.'

An insight into the life of a bearded gentleman in the 17th century is given in *Pylades and Corinna* (1731), which is a biography of Mrs William Thomas. A description of her grandfather, Richard Shute, runs: 'He was very nice in the mode of that age, his valet being some hours every morning in starching his beard and curling his whiskers, during which time a gentleman whom he maintained as a companion was always ready to read to him upon some useful subject.'

Once the beard and moustache had been trimmed, the Elizabethan gentleman expected them to be perfumed, or dusted with powdered orris root, or starched. They could be spun into ringlets with curling irons, and they were frequently dyed. A famous comment on different coloured beards of the time occurs in Shakespeare's *A Midsummer Night's Dream*, where Bottom offers to play the part of Pyramus in 'either your straw-colour beard, your orange-tawny beard, your purple-in-grain beard, or your French-crown colour beard, your perfect yellow'.

The Tudors and Stuarts certainly perfected the art of beard-wearing, developing a wide range of styles. They also came up with the ideal collar to set off a beard, the ruff. Beard enthusiasts should think seriously of reviving it!

One of the best-known remarks in history is that of Francis Drake, as reported by Francis Bacon: 'I remember Drake, in the vaunting style of a soldier, would call the Enterprise [of Cadiz, 1587] the

Sir Francis Drake (1540?–96) with a pique-devant or bodkin.

he was to be executed or not. He said that there was a law-suit pending between himself and the king, respecting his head, and until the matter was settled the beard should not be touched. Raleigh was eventually executed on 29 October 1618.

There is a famous anecdote concerning Sir Thomas More, who was executed on 6 July 1535. He had been found guilty of high treason, though his principal crime seems to have been to oppose the divorce of Henry VIII. As he laid his head on the block, Sir Thomas carefully moved his long beard to one side. 'Let my beard be spared,' he said. 'It, at least, has not offended the king.'

singeing of the King of Spain's beard.' Sellars and Yeatman, in *1066 And All That*, later referred to the king's beard as the Spanish Mane.

Sir Walter Raleigh refused to have his beard trimmed while he was waiting to learn whether

THE 18TH CENTURY

In Queen Anne's time beards and moustaches went completely out of fashion. Those men who could afford to do so wore wigs of white or grey artificial hair. A bearded chin beneath such a wig would have looked absurd.

Beards have not been the norm in western countries since the beginning of the 20th century. A return to a bearded period has several times been predicted, in the 1960s, for example, when the hippies appeared on the scene, and more recently when designer stubble appeared to be gaining ground, but it has not yet happened. Some would say that with the influence of women becoming stronger every year, it is unlikely that beards will ever come back into general favour.

Another factor is that there

Sir Walter Raleigh (1552?–1618) with a Pisa or stiletto.

seems to be no one around in modern times who feels passionate enough about beards to campaign vigorously for them. Not that a one-man crusade would be likely to produce much result. During the last beardless period, which overlapped both ends of the 18th century, Dulaure tried to persuade his countrymen to stop shaving. In 1786 he wrote, optimistically: 'The fashion of long beards is on the point of being renewed, an epoch which I pronounce to be nearer than people think. All our present fashions and customs are nothing more than old ones revived, which will disappear in their turn. The revolution is just at an end: the rapidity of our changes has accelerated its course, and a new reign is at hand.

'You pretty fellows of the present day, Jemmy-Jessamy parsons, jolly bucks, and all you with smock faces and weak nerves, be dumb with astonishment: I foretell it, you will soon resemble men.' The words were brave enough, but another 50 years were to pass before the prophecy was fulfilled.

THE 19TH CENTURY

An eloquent defender of the beard was the Englishman Robert Southey (1774–1843), poet laureate. The surprising thing was that Southey himself was clean-shaven. It is hard to imagine why when you read his enthusiastic comments. 'I myself, if I wore a beard, should cherish it, as the Cid Campeador did, for my pleasure. I should regale it on a summer's day with rose water, and without making it an idol, I should sometimes offer incense to it, with a pastille, or with lavender and sugar. My children, when they were young enough for such blandishments, would have delighted to stroke and comb and curl it, and my grandchildren in their turn would have succeeded to the same course of mutual endearment.' (The point Southey makes about young children playing with a parental beard seems to indicate that he had observed such behaviour and been touched by it.)

Yet another 19th-century defence of the beard appeared in the *Irish Quarterly*. To the more ribald eye of the 20th century, some of the writer's comments seem a little ambiguous. Remember that it is the beard he is discussing when he says: 'Why should men cut off what nature has given them for use, comfort, and ornament, and as a distinguishing characteristic of their sex!' The beard, continued this enthusiast, was not only ornamental, but conveyed the 'idea of strength, decision, manliness, depth of intellect, solidity — in short, everything may be said in its favour — nothing against it'.

So saying, the writer nonetheless then proceeded to imagine what women might say against it, which was that their bearded menfolk might look like nasty Frenchmen. 'Certainly not!' he exclaimed. 'If we ceased to shave, we should not cease to use soap and water, and I venture to say that the English beard would be the cleanest, glossiest, handsomest thing in the world.'

The English and the French have always tended to laugh at one another's strange habits. In 1844 an article in *New Monthly Magazine* had this to say: 'They seem more disposed to slaughter others than to shave themselves. When a party of young Frenchmen approach one, it is like the advance of a herd of goats. We never remember our neighbours so irritable as they are at present. The reason is obvious; they were never so exposed to be plucked by the beard. Fortunately, it is easier just now for England to pluck France by the beard than for France to return the affront. We are still respectable and razored.'

The writer of the article may well have been respectably razored, but if he continued to be respectable, he was no doubt bearded 10 years later. Whether the English followed French fashion is unclear, but by the 1850s beards were once again very much part of the English social scene.

It has been suggested that the Crimean War was responsible for reintroducing beards to Victorian England. G M Trevelyan states in his *English Social History*: 'The Crimean War had also its effects in lesser matters. In imitation of our heroes in the trenches before Sebastopol, smoking became fashionable again after being banished from polite circles for eighty years. For the same reason beards returned

after an absence from well-bred societies of two centuries. The typical mid-Victorian of all classes was a man with a beard and a pipe.' However, there are cartoons in contemporary issues of *Punch* magazine which seem to indicate that beards had begun to return rather earlier than the mid-1850s.

Middle-aged men sometimes have difficulty adjusting to the new fashions for the young, but it must have been especially difficult for men who were middle-aged at that time. They had grown up used to the sight of military men with their side-whiskers and curled mustachios, but civilians had always been clean-shaven, and even the military were beardless. England had in fact been virtually without beards for 150 years, yet they now suddenly began to appear. Perhaps something of the same shock was felt by middle-aged and older men in the 1960s, when once again beards were seen after a long period of absence.

In the mid-19th century discussions about the pros and cons of beards appeared in almost every newspaper and magazine. Editors were faced with the problem of whether to be openly in favour of the beard's return, thereby possibly offending those readers who still objected to it, or condemning beards and annoying those readers who had just decided to grow one. A certain amount of sitting on the fence was called for, and was brilliantly achieved by the *Westminster Review*: '[The beard] being an object of so much interest and dispute just now is profoundly natural. We approach the subject with the impartiality of Cicero's friends at the New Academy. All that we can claim is freedom from tyranny on the one side and, on the other, that he who wears a beard and he who rejects it may equally be permitted liberty of conscience. So that we neither advocate nor do we oppose its adoption.'

The author of this article nevertheless went on to flatter indirectly those readers who did decide to grow a beard: 'As certain dresses do not become diminutive women and must, in order to display their wonted effect be worn by those of noble stature, so the beard — identified as it is with sternness, dignity and strength — is only the becoming complement of true manliness. If we are not mistaken, therefore, the cultivation of the beard is a perilous experiment for all degenerate sons of Adam and may produce in the wearers the most ludicrous incongruity. We trust that the noble association with the beard will never be degraded, and we would advise all beard-loving aspirants to be well assured of their worthiness — physically and mentally — to wear it before they show themselves in a decoration so significant of honour.'

The writer was well aware that his self-satisfied readers would have no doubts about their own claim to the 'worthiness' he talked about.

John Waters, who wrote for a magazine called *Knickerbocker*,

was not, to put it mildly, a philopogonist. He began quietly, with an indirect swipe at moustaches, but it was not long before his disgust for beards made itself known:

'I would not object to the soft, silky, well-trained moustache of one of our leisurely lads who has nothing else to do in the world but attend to his toilette and spend gracefully the money that his father acquired and perhaps went to the devil for, and I might well admire a pair of moustaches like those of the late renowned Ali Pasha of Egypt that were taught to grow upward, diminishing in volume, until the fine master-hairs of the ends mingled with the long lashes of his brilliant eyes, but to see our yard-wide men, who in their youth have never imagined a beard at full-length except upon a maniac or a religious enthusiast coming forth in this community of sober merchants with their strait, stiff, red or pepper-and-salt bristles, occupying the thoughts of peaceful men and disgusting *ad nauseam* those of a more refined class, is an enormity no longer to be endured in silence.'

The writer went on to describe a man 'that it is my mischance to be acquainted with, who wears a red stiff brush at the extremity of his chin, of the very hue and wiry consistency of the beard of Judas Iscariot'.

Waters returned to the attack a month later in another article. Its essential message was: 'There exists no right whatever to exhibit to the community a disgusting object of this sort;

Emperor of France, Napoleon III (1808–73) with an Imperial, or Napoleon III beard; sometimes called a royale.

restored to pristine dignity as the artistic cultivator of man's distinguishing appendage. Already the martial moustache, the haughty imperial, and the daily expanding whiskers, like accredited heralds, proclaim the approaching advent of the monarch Beard; the centuries of his banishment are drawing to their destined close, and the hour and the man are at hand to re-establish his ancient reign.'

'Perennial pilosity' could hardly be bettered as a description of a long-term beard, but there is that favourite 19th-century phrase again — 'man's distinguishing appendage'.

The Westminster Review was also rather ambiguous, as well as being out of touch with what was happening at the time, when it commented in 1854 that the beard in Europe 'is at present in what we must venture to call an unnatural position'. This did not mean that beards were no longer being grown on men's faces, under their chins, merely that their position in society had changed. A beard, said the writer, had once been the 'symbol of patriarch and king; it is now, it would seem, that of revolution, democracy and dissatisfaction with existing institutions. Conservatism and respectability shave close.'

This is an astonishing comment, given the date. The writer of the article is really describing the situation that existed in the early part of the 19th century when he says of the beard that 'all kinds of offices discourage or prohibit it;

upon every principle of comity and social order they ought to be abolished. Trim your Imperials. Subdue your Moustaches. Banish your Beards.'

Tait's *Edinburgh Magazine* also tackled the subject. It was fairly safe in prophesying that beards would soon be fashionable again, since it only made that announcement when there was ample evidence on all sides that they were indeed coming back. But if not especially far-seeing, the writer of the following is still to be congratulated for his fine phrases: 'We have had visions of things looming in the future and we are enabled to prophesy that beards are coming back again. Civilized chins shall again repose in the shadow of perennial pilosity; and the barber, no longer condemned to reap the barren crop of a stubble field, shall be

Lord Alfred Tennyson (1809–92) with a full beard.

only a few travellers, artists, men of letters and philosophers wear it.'

However, the writer thought this to be an 'unnatural' situation. This was clearly the generally held view, and for the next 50 years a beard became a distinctive feature of the respectable Victorian gentleman.

Many of the eminent Victorians, such as Dickens, Tennyson, Darwin, Browning, are all known to us as richly bearded men. Most of their portraits were painted in later life, after they had achieved fame. There do exist earlier portraits of Dickens and Tennyson, showing them in their clean-shaven state. Some critics have remarked that it was a pity that they subsequently hid such fine faces behind the obligatory beard. We would naturally argue that fine faces merely act as a good foundation for fine beards.

In the 1890s, some young men who wished to show how independent they were did so by not growing a beard. Oscar Wilde, Aubrey Beardsley and Max Beerbohm were amongst the young dandies who turned away from the imposing beards that were all around them. They were the ones, perhaps, who began the present-day preference for clean-shaven faces. That fashion, of course, now means that young men have to grow beards in order to rebel.

Of the beards worn by American presidents, the best known is probably that of President Lincoln, perhaps because he was the first president to wear one. Even he was clean-shaven before his election. He is said to have grown his beard at the suggestion of a little girl called Grace Bedell, of Westfield, New York. President Grant had what has been called a 'short and utilitarian' beard, though that begs the question of how exactly a beard can have a practical use. Rutherford Hayes had a long and flowing beard,

Abraham Lincoln (1809–65) with the beard style later called Lincolnic.

James Garfield a bushy one, Chester A Arthur sprightly whiskers. The last presidential beard was that of Benjamin Harrison. It is said to have had both charm and dignity.

Lewis Gannet has reported that Harvard University students of the 1870s were bewhiskered. As the century wore on the beards disappeared, leaving only the moustaches. In the class of 1900 there were no beards.

The great evolutionist Charles Darwin (1809–82) with a full or flowing beard. A cartoon by 'E.W.'.

6   *Bookish beards*

For those of you whose intellectual-looking beards are not just there for show, we are about to tackle the subject of The Beard in Literature, and even The Beard in Art. Charles Dickens, for example, has a piece called *The Ghost of Art*. It makes fun of contemporary fashions in painting, especially 'the German taste'. Dickens describes a meeting with a male model who, for professional reasons, grows a 'long dark beard, curling over his upper lip, twisting about the corners of his mouth, and hanging down upon his breast'.

According to Dickens, the model is highly successful, arranging his beard in different ways for different artists. 'The man might have left his face alone, or had no face. The beard did everything.'

On this same subject of the beard in art, God the Father, in religious paintings of the Renaissance period, is nearly always shown as an old man with a long beard. Some commentators have suggested that because a beard hides part of the face, it is suggestive of mystery, a necessary attribute of God. The beard also manages to suggest wisdom.

On a connected theme, there is this little poem by Aldous Huxley:

> Christlike in my behaviour,
> Like every good believer,
> I imitate the saviour
> And cultivate a beaver.

That was written in the 1920s, when everyone would have recognized that a 'beaver' was a beard. Many other commentators have pointed out that Jesus Christ set an example for his followers by being bearded. That, at least, is the assumption, and how artists have seen Christ through the centuries. Whether the fact that artists themselves have often been bearded has anything to do with it is difficult to say.

In a more secular context, it must be frustrating for the beautiful women whose faces adorn advertising posters in public places to see what happens to their faces once they are displayed. If their teeth can be seen, one or two of them will almost certainly have been blacked out. The same folk artist will probably also have had the 'original' idea of giving them a moustache and beard.

The only consolation one can offer the victims is to say that the pogonic additions, at least, merely emphasize their femininity. The woman who has suffered most in this respect is Mona Lisa. Marcel Duchamp, in 1919, seems to have been the first to display a version of the famous painting with a moustache and beard added to it. The image has since become familiar, the lady concerned smiling serenely through it all.

POGONIC PROSE

Some writers can be quite lyrical in their descriptions of beards. Here, for instance, is Saul Bellow talking about Rabbi Sandor-Alexander Herzog in his novel *Herzog*. 'He wore a beautiful beard as well, a radiant, broad-strung beard that hid the outline of his chin and also the velvet collar of his frock coat. Herzog's mother had had a weakness for Jews with handsome beards. In her family, too, all the elders had beards that were thick and rich, full of religion.'

Later Bellow refers to 'foaming beards', and describes the bowler-hatted elders 'who gave their beards a finger-combing'.

Another literary description of a beard occurs in *Whisky Galore*, by Compton Mackenzie. Cameron of Kilwhillie is said to have 'a monster of a beard breaking below his nose like a wave on the Skerryvore'.

Robert Penn Warren, in his novel *Night Rider*, gives us a detailed portrait of one of his characters: 'There was scarcely any gray in Professor Ball's scraggly, red-brown beard which sprang in tangled tufts from the bony chin and cheeks, like vegetation that hardily finds a foothold on an arid and rocky hillside.'

This is hardly an imposing beard, and might have been of that type which manages to irritate other people. 'I do not recognise your face, but I remember the cut of your beard, which I have the misfortune to dislike. Here, sir, is a sovereign; which I very willingly advance to you on the single condition that you shave your chin.' This little speech occurs in *The Dynamiter*, by Robert Louis Stevenson. It recalls Shakespeare's *As You Like It*, where Touchstone explains why

Captain Kettle's 'torpedo' beard. Illustration by Stanley Wood, 1898, for The Adventures of Captain Kettle *by C J Cutliffe Hyne.*

he was involved in a quarrel by saying: 'I did dislike the cut of a certain courtier's beard . . .'

In one of his short stories, *The Last Trump*, H G Wells jokes about the effect of a bewhiskered face by saying of a character: 'He had the face of a saint, but he had rendered this generally acceptable by growing side-whiskers.'

Whiskers are often described as 'bushy'. P G Wodehouse extended the metaphor. In Usborne's *Wodehouse At Work* he is quoted as saying: 'The station-master's whiskers are of a Victorian bushiness and give the impression of having been grown under glass.'

Daisy Ashford's book *The Young Visiters*, written in 1890 when she was nine years old and first published in 1919, has charmed many a child and adult reader alike. Daisy tells us, in her uncorrected spelling, that her Mr Salteena 'had dark short hair and mustache and wiskers which were very black and twisty'.

'He had a thin vague beard, or rather he had a chin on which large numbers of hairs weakly curled and clustered to cover its retreat.' This is quoted by S C Roberts in his book about Max Beerbohm, *The Incomparable Max*.

Laurence Sterne, in his whimsical novel *Tristram Shandy*, remarks in passing: 'How Homer could write with so long a beard, I don't know.'

In *The Spectator* (No. 331) Addison says that his friend Sir Roger de Coverley, pointing to the bust of a venerable old man, asked him whether he did not think 'our ancestors looked much wiser in their beards than we without them. For my part, when I am walking in my gallery in the country, and see my ancestors, who many of them died before they were my age, I cannot forbear regarding them as so many patriarchs, and at the same time looking upon myself as an idle, smock-faced young fellow. I love to see your Abrahams, your Isaacs and your Jacobs, with beards below their girdles, that cover half the hangings.'

Jonathan Swift was, as always, more cynical. In his *Thoughts on Various Subjects* he writes: 'Old men and comets have been reverenced for the same reason; their long beards, and pretences to foretell events.'

POGONIC POEMS

Poems about beards have rarely been of high literary quality, but many of them are worth reading for other reasons. Most of the verses were written in the great age of the beard, from 1550 to 1650.

John Taylor (1578–1653), usually known as 'The Water Poet', was hardly a great literary craftsman, but his doggerel verses are of considerable antiquarian interest. He was bearded himself, at one time sporting a so-called screw beard, but he was also an observer of other people's beards. The following lines are from his *Superbiae Flagellum*, otherwise called *The Whip of Pride*:

'Now a few lines to paper I

will put,
Of men's beards' strange and variable cut,
In which there's some do take as vain a pride,
As almost in all other things beside.
(And in my time of some men I have heard,
Whose wisdom have been only wealth and beard;)
Many of these the proverb well doth fit,
Which says — bush natural, more hair than wit.
Some seem as they were starched and fine,
Like to the bristles of some angry swine;
And some (to let their loves' desire on edge),
Are cut and prun'd like to a quickset hedge.
Some like a spade, some like a fork, some square,
Some round, some mow'd like stubble, some stark bare,
Some sharp, stiletto fashion, dagger-like,
That may with whispering a man's eyes outpike:
Some with the hammer cut, or Roman T,
Their beards extravagant reformed must be,
Some with the quadrate, some triangle fashion,
Some circular, some oval in translation,
Some perpendicular in longitude,
Some like a thicket for their crassitude,
That heights, depths, breadths, triform, square, oval, round,
And rules geometrical in beards are found.'

John Taylor, 'The Water Poet' (1578–1653) with a rare example of a screw beard.

Taylor continued with some remarks about moustaches, which we quote in the chapter on that subject. (For the various beard styles mentioned in the poem, see Words Bewhiskered, p. 115.)

A man called Barnes wrote a *Defence of the Beard* in doggerel verse in the 16th century, apparently in answer to an attack on the beard by Andrew Borde, a physician in the time of Henry VIII. Barnes's style is illustrated below:

'But, syr, I praye you, yf you tell can,
Declare to me when God made man,
(I meane by our forefather Adam)
Whyther he had a berde than;
And yf he had, who dyd hym shave,
Syth that a barber he coulde not have.'

Later in the poem Barnes compares 'new shavyd men' to 'scraped swyne'.

In *Satirical Songs and Poems on Costume*, edited by F W Fairholt for the Percy Society, an anonymous *Ballad of the Beard* is reprinted. It dates from the early 17th century and comments on the variety of beard cuts that were prevalent at the time. The opening verse implies that beards had been under attack. This may refer to Puritan comments. There is also an interesting hint that some cuts of beard had become associated with particular professions:

The beard, thick or thin, on
  the lip or the chin,
Doth dwell so near the
  tongue,
That her silence in the beard's
  defence
May do her neighbour wrong.

Now a beard is a thing that
  commands in a king,
Be his sceptre ne'er so fair:
Where the beard bears the
  sway the people obey,
And are subject to a hair.

'Tis a princely sight, and a
  grave delight,
That adorns both young and
  old;
A well-thatcht face is a
  comely grace,
And a shelter from the cold.

When the piercing north
  comes thundering forth,
Let a barren face beware;
For a trick it will find, with a
  razor of wind,
To shave a face that's bare.

Now of beards there be such
  company,
And fashions such a throng,
That it's very hard to handle a
  beard,
Tho' it be never so long.

The Roman T, in its bravery,
Doth first itself disclose,
But so high it turns, that oft it
  burns
With the flames of a torrid
  nose.

The stiletto beard, oh, it
  makes me afeard,
It is so sharp beneath,
For he that doth place a
  dagger in's face,
What wears he in his sheath?

But, methinks, I do itch to go
  thro' the stitch
The needle beard to amend,
Which, without any wrong, I
  may call too long,
For a man can see no end.

The soldier's beard doth
  march in shear'd,
In figure like a spade,
With which he'll make his
  enemies quake,
And think their graves are
  made.

What doth invest a bishop's
  breast,
But a milk-white spreading
  hair?
Which an emblem may be of
  integrity
Which doth inhabit there.

But oh, let us tarry for the
  beard of King Harry,
That grows about the chin,
With his bushy pride, and a
  grove on each side,
And a champion ground
  between.

Hudibras, by Samuel Butler, is a satire in the form of a mock-heroic poem. It was published in the 17th century and ridicules the hypocrisy of the Presbyterians and Independents of the time. The hero is a pedantic Presbyterian who has a portentous beard:

> His tawny beard was th'equal grace
> Both of his wisdom and his face;
> In cut and dye so like a tile,
> A sudden view it would beguile:
> The upper part whereof was whey,
> The nether orange mixed with grey.
> This hairy meteor did denounce
> The fall of sceptres and of crowns
> With grisly type did represent
> Declining age of government . . .

The person being mocked was probably Philip Nye, an Independent minister famous for his unusual beard. Samuel Butler seems to have taken great exception to it: he makes insulting remarks about it in several of his poems. One poem is entirely devoted to the beard, and begins:

> A beard is but the vizard of the face,
> That nature orders for no other place;
> The fringe and tassel of the countenance
> That hides his person from another man's.

Elsewhere Butler writes:

> This reverend brother, like a goat,
> Did wear a tail upon his throat;
> The fringe and tassel of a face,
> That gives it a becoming grace,
> But set in such a curious frame,
> As if 'twere wrought in filograin;
> And cut so even as if't had been
> Drawn with a pen upon the chin.

THE BARD AND BEARDS

Shakespeare, bearded himself, makes over 90 direct references to them in his plays, together with other allusions to shaving, visits to the barber, etc. In *All's Well That Ends Well*, for instance, the countess tells the clown that he has given an answer that fits all questions. The clown replies that 'it is like a barber's chair, that fits all buttocks.'

'I must to the barber's, monsieur,' says Bottom, in *A Midsummer Night's Dream*, 'for methinks I am marvellous hairy about the face.' He is indeed, having been given the head of an ass by Oberon.

In *Antony and Cleopatra* we are told that 'our courteous Antony . . . being barber'd ten times o'er, goes to the feast'. *1 Henry IV* has a contemptuous reference by Hotspur to 'a certain lord, neat and trimly dress'd, fresh as a bridegroom, and his chin new reap'd show'd like a stubble land at harvest home'.

Rosalind tells Orlando, in *As You Like It*, that he cannot be in love: 'There is none of my uncle's marks upon you; he taught me how to know a man in love; in which cage of rushes I am sure you are not his prisoner.' 'What were his marks?' asks Orlando. 'A lean cheek, which you have not; a blue eye and sunken, which you have not; an unquestionable spirit, which you have not; a beard neglected, which you have not; but I pardon you for that.'

In *The Merchant of Venice*, Old Gobbo does not recognize his son when he meets him after a long absence, thanks to the beard which Launcelot now wears: 'I'll be sworn, if thou be Launcelot, thou art mine own flesh and blood. Lord worshipped might he be, what a beard hast thou got! Thou hast got more hair on thy chin than Dobbin my fill-horse has on his tail.'

On the question of playing Shakespearean roles, Tallulah Bankhead writes in her autobiography (*Tallulah*, 1952): 'Alec Guinness, one of the most brilliant actors of our time, in 1951 set himself up as Hamlet in London. Mr Guinness is a thinker as well as an actor—a fusion encountered as seldom as Halley's comet. After much consideration, he decided to play the Dane with a beard. He won't do it again. The hue and cry was deafening . . . You can't play ducks and drakes with tradition in England. Had David Garrick or Sir Henry Irving or Beerbohm Tree profaned Hamlet with whiskers? No! Then let's have no more of such hanky-panky!'

One should add to this the comment that Sir Alec was certainly right to suggest that a real-life Dane of Hamlet's time would have been bearded.

All Elizabethan dramatists, not just Shakespeare, could be relied upon to comment satirically on the excesses of the time. They obviously thought that barbers were making their profession more complex than it needed to be. In his *Midas* (1591), for instance, John Lyly has a barber ask a customer: 'How, sir, will you be trimmed? Will you have your beard like a spade or a bodkin (i.e. a dagger)? A pent-house (i.e. a shed with a sloping roof) on your upper lip, or an alley on your chin? A low curl on your head like a bull, or dangling lock like a spaniel? Your mustachios sharp at the ends like shoemakers' awls, or hanging down to your mouth like goats' flakes? Your love-locks wreathed with a silken twist, or shaggy to fall on your shoulders?'

HUMOROUS POEMS

Perhaps some of the poems quoted earlier were humorous in their day, causing many a 16th- or 17th-century reader to roll about in the aisle, but most modern readers will prefer something like this—an anonymous little poem quoted in *Oddities and Curiosities of Words and Literature*, by C C Bombaugh:

> With whiskers thick upon my face
> I went my fair to see;
> She told me she could never

love
A bear-faced chap like me.

I shaved them clean and
    called again,
And thought my troubles
    o'er;
She laughed outright, and
    said I was
More bare-faced than before.

That is a nice little joke, but it raises a slightly more serious question. If clean-shaven faces are thought to be more open and frank than those concealed behind beards, why do we speak about a 'bare-faced' lie? What seems to have happened is that bare-faced, apart from its literal meaning, was at first applied generally to behaviour that was unconcealed or undisguised. From there it went on to mean shameless, impudent. The phrase 'bare-faced lie' itself seems first to have been used in *Uncle Tom's Cabin*, by Harriet Beecher Stowe.

You will be familiar with Edward Lear's famous limerick about beards. It appears in the *Book of Nonsense*.

There was an old man with a
    beard
Who said: 'It is just as I
    feared —
Two Owls and a Hen,
Four Larks and a Wren
Have all built their nests in
    my beard.'

Lear's limerick is referred to in the following verses, which was discovered in *Our Man at Saint Withits* (1964), by S J Forrest. The poem was apparently inspired by a news item that read: 'Christians from all over the world make pilgrimage to the Patriarch of Constantinople to be enveloped in his welcoming beard.'

Our clergyman sports a
    luxuriant beard,
In the style of the Orthodox
    East;
He rears it on compost and
    liquid manure,
In a foaming solution of yeast.

He claims that his whiskers
    are wholly inspired,
And his yearning for unity
    cheered,
By the Constantinopolitanian
    pope,
With his lush and benevolent
    beard.

'My Aaronic foliage, dripping
    with oil,
Should patently serve to
    impart
A pleasant aroma of brotherly
    love,
From a warm, ecumenical
    heart.

81

'The fine ornithophorous fuzz
    of the man
Who said, "It is just as I
    feared,"
Is precisely the end that I
    hope to achieve
In the warmth of a welcoming
    beard.

'The birds in this case, that
    my whiskers embrace,
Are Baptists and Methodists,
    too,
Salvationists, Orthodox,
    Romanists, Friends,
Besides the occasional Jew.

'And thus, in a measure, I
    shall without fail,
The cause of reunion push;
By methods embracing the
    bird in the hand,
And numberless birds in the
    bush.'

COBBLERS

Since we began this chaper with
Dickens, we thought we would
end with him. That naturally
made us think of cobblers. In
The Pickwick Papers we find 'He
was a sallow man —all cobblers
are; and had a strong, bristly
beard —all cobblers have.' Is
that still true of the cobbling
fraternity?

Elsewhere, in one of his
brilliantly evocative thumbnail
sketches the author describes
Matthew Bagnet, a minor
character in *Bleak House*, as 'tall
and upright, with shaggy
eyebrows, and whiskers like the
fibres of a cocoanut, not a hair
upon his head, and a torrid
complexion. Voice, short, deep
and resonant, not at all unlike
the tones of the instrument
(bassoon) to which he is
devoted.'

In addition to his cocoanut-
fibre whiskers (wonderful!), Mr
Bagnet has a wife who rules
over him, though he will never
admit it, and three children
named Malta, Quebec and
Woolwich, because they
happened to be born in those
places. Perhaps Woolwich, as
the only boy of the trio, grew up
to have the same cocoanut-fibre
beard as his father.

There was an Old Man in a tree,
Whose Whiskers were lovely to see;
    But the Birds of the Air
    Pluck'd them perfectly bare,
To make themselves nests in that tree.

7 A bevy of beavers

If ever there was a trivial pursuit, long before those Canadians made a fortune from a board game of that name, it was Beaver. Beaver was the great beard-spotting game of the 1920s, played mostly by undergraduates at the universities of Oxford and Cambridge. Bear in mind that students of that time would all have been clean-shaven, having been born after 1900. Around them would have been the bearded survivals of the late Victorian era, men who had lived through a bearded age and were reluctant to part with their foliage.

The game of Beaver began as an irreverent comment by the young on those Victorian left-overs. In its simplest form the game was played by two or more young men who shouted 'Beaver!' whenever they saw a bearded man. The first one to do so scored a point. For some reason the scoring system adopted was that of tennis, so the first beard spotted would result in a score of 15–0.

Some played more refined versions of the game. In a letter to the *Daily Telegraph* in 1987, Mark Bence-Jones, of Ipswich, gave details of how his late father had played the game while at Cambridge. Red Beavers and Royal Beavers scored extra points. Spotting a Red Beaver riding a green bicycle immediately won the game. A Royal Beaver riding a green bicycle won game and set. The highest possible score in the game would have been achieved by spotting a Female Red Royal Beaver riding a green bicycle.

The game had that special brand of silliness which has always appealed to male English undergraduates, but it did not last long. The Opies, in their *Lore and Language of Schoolchildren*, remarked that the cry of 'Beaver!' was a thing of the past, replaced in modern times, if at all, by shouts of 'Beardie!' or 'Fungus Face!'. As for Beaver itself, the name of the game, most people would have associated it with the rodent. It seems, though, that there could have been a more learned allusion to the lower part of the face-guard of a helmet. In this meaning 'beaver' derives from Old French *baviere*, a child's bib, which in turn derives from *bave*, 'saliva'.

Beaver took on various senses. The word could refer to

Ambrose Everett Burnside, American General (1824–81) whose distinctive mutton chop whiskers became known in the US as burnsides. Later this name turned back to front, and now as sideburns applies to any long, straight side-whiskers, such as those worn here by Elvis Presley (1935–77).

the game, or to a beard, or to a bearded man. 'See the beaver with a medal,' says a young girl to another, in Evelyn Waugh's *Vile Bodies*. 'Who is that very important young man?' asks the other. Already in 1910 Frank Richardson, in his *Whiskers and Soda*, had written: 'He provided a list of celebrated clean-shaven men and also of celebrated beavers, as bearded men are technically termed.'

The game of beaver-spotting could well be revived. It is a pleasant pastime, as easily practised while commuting or walking through a crowded street as when lazily watching the world go by from a café table or in a pub. A 19th-century observer had this to say:

'Let us take the next half-dozen men passing the window as we write. The first has his whiskers tucked into the corners of his mouth as though he were holding them up with his teeth. The second whisker that we descry has wandered into the middle of the cheek, and there stopped, as though it did not know where to go, like a youth who has ventured out into the middle of a ball-room with all eyes upon him. Yonder bunch of bristles twists the contrary way, under the owner's ears; he could not, for the life of him, tell why it retrograded so. The fourth citizen, with the vast Pacific of a face, has little whiskers, which seem to have stopped short after two inches of voyage, as though aghast at the prospect of having to double such a Cape Horn of a chin. We perceive coming a tremendous pair, running over the shirt in luxuriant profusion.'

BAGGING BEARDS

Frank Richardson, whose works have already been quoted frequently, must have kept a beard-spotter's diary. He pretended to dislike beards and whiskers, but was obviously fascinated by them. To quote him once more, on the subject of beards and fog—which gets into a beard, making it damp—in his *Whiskers and Soda* Richardson suggested that on such days bearded men should 'wear the waterproof whisker-bags that they use for motoring'.

Having made his useful suggestion about beard bags—one that all bearded men who venture forth on foggy days will appreciate—Frank Richardson rather spoilt things by adding: 'Even if fog were bad for whiskers, anything that is bad for whiskers is good for humanity.'

BEARDS AND BEARDS

And now a selection of the many anecdotes and stories that were encountered during the research of this book:

There is a town in western Illinois which sounds as if it has hairy male inhabitants. It is called Beardstown. It was actually named after a certain Thomas Beard, who settled there in 1819. (The town's chief claim to fame is that in a murder trial which took place in 1858, Abraham Lincoln was the defence counsel. He won an acquittal for the defendant.)

One of the countless anecdotes told of the famous conductor Sir Thomas Beecham, who had a fine beard, concerns a rehearsal with the London Symphony Orchestra. Sir Thomas noted that the violins were inclined to follow the leader, Paul Beard, rather than himself: 'Look at me, not at the leader,' he told them. 'There are two beards here. May I suggest that you pay a little more attention to this beard.'

In the western world, as mentioned earlier, a beard may on occasion cause a man to be addressed by a generic nickname, such as Beardie or Whiskers. In a country like Jordan, the wearing of a beard can also affect the manner in which a man is addressed. If he is bearded he is assumed to be a faithful Moslem, entitled to be addressed politely as 'sheikh'. The honorific is granted only to

Sir Thomas Beecham (1879–1961).

a bearded man — a moustache would not be enough.

According to Peter Walton, a BBC executive television producer, he gets very good service in Chinese restaurants because he wears a beard. 'The Chinese associate beards with wisdom,' he says, and they respect wise men.

Beards have indeed long been associated with wisdom, usually the wisdom of old age, but many writers have pointed out that the mere fact of having a beard does not convert a man into an intellectual. One of the more acid comments was by the Greek Ammianus. His epigram runs: 'A beard creates lice, not brains.'

To pull, or cut off, or harm in any way a man's beard was the deadliest of insults in ancient times. In the Old Testament (2 Sam. 10ff) the story is told of Hanun, King of the Ammonites, who made the mistake of insulting David's servants. He created a new beard style for them by cutting off half their beards. Hanun's advisers had told him that David's men were spies, though in fact they had been sent by David to offer sympathy for the death of the King's father. The insult was later avenged in battle, the Ammonites suffering a total defeat.

Members of the present British royal family have occasionally been seen in beards, especially while serving in the Royal Navy, but they otherwise remain clean-shaven. Queen Elizabeth II is reported to have disliked the full-set that Prince Charles twice grew

Prince Philip, Duke of Edinburgh, bearded in 1945 during his naval days.

during his naval service, though one of her favourite portraits of the Duke of Edinburgh is said to show him as a bearded young naval officer.

Douglas Slocombe, who worked with veteran British film director Charles Crichton on many of his Ealing comedies, says that Crichton sometimes gets involved in real-life comedy. He described how he, Crichton and a bearded composer went to a restaurant after a music session, only to hear three rowdies at the next table loudly laughing about men with beards. Crichton took a bottle of soy sauce and poured it over the head of one of the loud-mouths, saying: 'And I don't like clean-shaven men.' In the fight that ensued, Crichton lost one of his front teeth.

Rudolph Valentino (born Rodolpho d'Antonguolla) was

the great romantic Hollywood film idol of the 1920s. His sudden death in 1925 at the age of 31 caused many suicides among his fans. The latter were mostly women, but a few young men of the time, hoping to be as attractive to women as he had been, copied the side-whiskers which were one of his trademarks. The fashion did not generally spread, becoming too closely associated with dance-hall gigolos.

George Santayana says in 'The British Character' in *Soliloquies of England*: 'Trust the man who hesitates in his speech and is quick and steady in action, but beware of long arguments and long beards.'

Rodolpho Alfonzo Rafaelo Pierre Filibert Guglielmi Di Valentina d'Antonguolla — better known to millions of adoring fans as Rudolph Valentino, with his distinctive side-whiskers or sideboards.

PROTRACTED POGONOLOGY

Beware of long beards indeed! Let us think about them for a moment. In some countries religious beliefs would prevent a trimming of the beard: there are also those who believe that an untrimmed beard is best for purely aesthetic reasons. As one anonymous writer expressed it in 1859, 'Nature is the best valet. Whiskers should never be curled nor pulled out to an absurd length. Still worse it is to cut them close.'

A writer in *Harper's Weekly* at the beginning of the present century agreed with that view. He said that the habit of trimming a beard or moustache 'caricatured the human countenance and reduced it more or less to a ridiculous burlesque of the honest visages of various sorts of animals'. A beard should be allowed to grow naturally, said the writer. A real beard was a full one. All other beards and moustaches he referred to interestingly as 'fragmentary forms'.

In the late 16th century, when the fashion in England and some other countries was for short, trimmed beards, the Germans seem to have favoured this idea of allowing the beard to reach its natural length. Andreas Eberhard Rauber von Talberg had a beard which was long enough to reach the ground and come back up to his belt. We are told that he went about on foot as often as possible so that people might admire it. Von Talberg walked with a staff, wrapping his beard

Hans Steiniger, Bürgermeister of Braunau, whose beard proved to be his downfall.

around it so that it would not drag along the ground. It is clear that he was no mere eccentric individual. 'Prolix' beards, as contemporary commentators on the German scene were fond of calling them, were clearly in general favour.

The next question has to be—how long is a long beard? *The Guinness Book of Records* naturally has something to say on the subject. The beard record, it seems, goes to Hans N Langseth, who was born in Norway in 1846. He spent the last 15 years of his life in the USA, and died in Iowa in 1927.

At the time of his death his beard measured 5.33 m *17½ft.* The beard was presented to the Smithsonian Institution, Washington, DC, in 1967. An Englishman called Richard Latter (1831–1914) reputedly had a beard which was 4.87 m *16 ft* long, but this is not verifiable.

Mention of these lengthy beards reminds us of a pogonic (see Words Bewhiskered p. 115, Word list) tragedy. It concerns a 16th-century official, the Bürgermeister of Branau, Austria. This official's name, in 1567, was Hans Steiniger (or in some records, Hannss Staininger). He was famous for the length of his beard, which extended to nearly 2.7 m *9 ft.* Since the Bürgermeister himself was considerably shorter than his beard, he normally tucked it around his waist as he moved about. One day he either forgot to do so, or it came loose. While he was ascending the staircase of the council chamber on 28 September 1567, he tripped over his beard, fell down the stairs, and was killed, victim of his own hairiness.

POLYCHROMATIC POGONOLOGY

Blackbeard—nickname of the ruthless pirate Edward Teach, killed 1718. According to legend he used to stick lighted matches in his long ragged black beard and hair to enhance his frightening appearance.

Bluebeard—in the *Tales* of Charles Parrault (1697) he is the chevalier Raoul, who entrusts his young wife with the keys of the castle. She is told that on no account should she go into a certain locked room. Inevitably her curiosity overcomes her and she does so, only to discover the skeletons of the chevalier's six former wives. The chevalier returns and is about to kill her when her brothers intervene and save her.

Many suggestions have been made as to the possible identity of the 'real' Bluebeard, but the basic tale of someone who disobeys an order because of curiosity, with unpleasant consequences, is ancient. It is unlikely that the story is true, or that it alludes to a real person.

Greybeard — used allusively of an old man. A greybeard is also a large earthenware or stoneware jug, used to hold spirits. It has a figure of a bearded man on it. 'Greybeards are always fond of blonde heads,' according to Victor Hugo. Many men have noticed that the hair of their beards turns grey before the hair on their heads turns that colour. Men with red hair are said to have beards which are several shades lighter in hue.

Orange-tawny beard — Bottom offers to wear a beard of this colour in Shakespeare's *Midsummer Night's Dream*.

Jules Dumont of France with his beard of 3.65 m 11 ft 11 in.

Red beard — Frederick I, Emperor of the Holy Roman Empire in the 12th century, was known by the nickname Barbarossa, 'red beard'.

White beard — Father Christmas is the automatic nickname for a man with a bushy white beard in England. In *A Dictionary of Nicknames*, Julian Franklyn reports that Santa is the American equivalent. Frank Richardson would have called such a beard a polar beaver.

The custom of dyeing beards was fairly common in the early 17th century, but the following remarks seem to indicate that the dyeing was not always well done, nor did it please everyone. The comments are taken from *The Artificial Changeling* (or *Anthropometamorphosis*), by John Bulwer, first published in 1650. The spelling has been modernized:

'Nor is the art of falsifying the natural hue of the beard wholly unknown to this more civilized part of the world; especially to old lechers who, knowing grey hairs in the beard to be a manifest sign of decay of the generative faculty, and an approaching impotency incident to age, vainly endeavour to obliterate the natural signification thereof.

'For there are some grown so foolish who being now grown old, decrepit, and unable for any kind of use or exercise, and this their weakness being notorious, and well known to all the world, and this their rotten building ready to fall; yet are they willing to deceive themselves, and everybody else (if they could), contrary to all truth and reason, by dyeing the hairs of their beards and heads, as if any man were so ignorant, and did not know that there are none of these changeable coloured beards, but at every motion of the sun, and every cast of the eye, they present a different colour, and never a one perfect, much like unto those in the necks of doves and pigeons: for in every hair of these old coxcombs you shall meet with three divers and sundry colours; white at the roots, yellow in the middle, and black at the point, like unto one of your parrot's feathers.'

POGONIC POT-POURRI

There is an old superstition that when boys and girls are present together at a baptism ceremony, the boys must be baptized first, otherwise they will grow up beardless. This probably would not matter much, but the same

Cuban Revolutionary: President Fidel Castro, nicknamed 'The Beard' by US Intelligence.

superstition says that the girls will have the beards instead.

Men with beards are more likely to be described as having a penetrating stare than are clean-shaven men. The charismatic gaze of Rasputin, the mad monk, is often mentioned in this connection. One possible explanation for the phenomenon is that a beard distracts attention away from the wearer's mouth, which is more sensual than spiritual, and focuses it on the eyes.

Does a man shape his beard according to his basic personality, or is he mainly influenced by the shape of his face and the way his beard happens to grow? Those in favour of the personality theory say that radicals and revolutionaries normally have shaggy, unkempt beards, that autocrats have short, pointed beards and that conventional types have well-trimmed, neat beards.

It was commonly believed in the past that the thickness of a man's beard was a direct indication of his virility. Making this point, an early writer called Theodoret said that removal of the beard is likely to make a man impotent. 'The greater or less quantity of beard a man has determines, in the same proportion, the vigour of his body.'

In *Boswell in Holland*, Frederick Pottle tells us that after his return from London in 1760 James Boswell founded at Edinburgh a jovial society

Rasputin, the mad monk (1871–1916).

known as the Soaping Club. In the jargon of his society, 'to soap a person's beard' meant to puff his vanity by flattery; to 'shave' him or 'to apply the razor' meant to deflate him with cutting wit.

A popular song in 1894, written by William Jerome with music by Andrew Mack, was called 'The Little Bunch of Whiskers on his Chin'. The opening lines were: 'A jay came to the city once, to see the funny sights, with a little bunch of whiskers on his chin.' In the slang of the time, 'jay' meant a simpleton, or greenhorn.

The Times could not resist reporting on the 17 barbershop owners who were arrested in Seoul in 1986. Between them they employed 87 women who, according to police, offered more than shaves to the customers. The story's appeal to the newspaper's sub-editor clearly lay in the headline that occurred to him. He headed the item 'Clip joints'. That phrase remains in use, though the slang meaning of 'to clip' — to overcharge someone — no longer seems to be current.

In *The Book of Similes* Robert Baldwin and Ruth Paris mention the anonymous reference to a bearded man who looked as if he 'was peering over a hedge'.

One of the beards that most adult Englishmen can visualize mentally is that of the legendary cricketer W G Grace. A G Steel has described him in action as a bowler (though he was more famous as a batsman): 'An enormous man rushing up to the wickets with both elbows out, a great black beard blowing on both sides of him, a huge yellow cap on top of a dark, swarthy face.'

The normally clean-shaven Romans allowed their beards to grow as a sign of mourning. The normally bearded ancient Greeks shaved off their beards for the same reason.

Nicholas Bentley, in his book *How Can You Bear To Be Human?*, advised any man who was growing a beard to make sure that it was house-trained — 'not such as will catch in the banisters or set fire to the face if exposed near a naked flame'.

Aaron's beard is a name applied to various plants, such as the

Dr W G Grace (1848–1915).

saxifrage, which is normally grown dangling from pots. The allusion is to Psalm 133. In early translations it refers to 'Aaron's beard, that went down to the skirts of his garments'. A more recent translation runs: 'Behold, how good and pleasant it is when brothers dwell in unity! It is like the precious oil upon the head, running down upon the beard, upon the beard of Aaron, running down on the collar of his robes!'

BEARDS IN BED

Men who wear beards for a long time become so accustomed to them that they almost forget their existence. There is a story about an elderly man with a long beard who was asked by his grandson what he did with the beard when he went to sleep at night. The old man told the boy that he had never thought about it, but would do so that night. When he went to bed that night he arranged his beard outside the sheets. Somehow that did not seem right, so he brought it inside the sheets. That was not right either. He spent a disturbed night, aware of his beard as he had never been before, and was still not able to answer his grandson next day.

This story reminds us of the Elizabethans who, because they sometimes starched and curled their beards, took special care of them at night. They often had pasteboard cases in which to enclose their beards, 'lest they should turn upon them and rumple them in their sleep'. They also had special beard combs and beard brushes for the daytime.

LAST WORDS

Chaucer refers in his *Canterbury Tales* to the custom of consecrating one's beard to a deity. In *The Knight's Tale* Arcite offers his beard to Mars:

> My berd, myn heer, that
>   hangeth long a doun,
> That neuer yit ne felt
>   offensioun

There was an Old Man with a beard,
Who sat on a horse when he reared;
But they said, 'Never mind! you will fall off behind,
You propitious Old Man with a beard!'

Of rasour ne of schere, I wol
  ye giue
And be thy trewe servaunt
  whiles I lyve.

A couple of anonymous
beard-twisters:

'A bearded peer on the pier
appeared to peer at his beard in
the pier glass.'

'I was barbarously barbarized
by the barbarity of a barbarian
barber in a barber's barbarizing
shop.'

In *Elsie Venner* Oliver Wendell
Holmes writes: 'When a
resolute young fellow steps up
to the great bully, the world,
and takes him boldly by the
beard, he is often surprised to
find that it comes off in his
hand, and that it was only tied
on to scare away timid
adventurers.'

The Sunday Correspondent, on
8 October 1989, ran a feature on
children's ideas about God.
Nearly all mentioned that he
had a beard, black, grey or
white. One child added that he
had a black moustache and was
about 12 feet tall.

The cartoonist and writer of
nonsense verse, Edward Lear,
grew a bushy beard in 1854
while he was travelling abroad.
He himself thought the beard
made him look like Henry VIII.
His biographer, Vivien Noakes,
says that he 'looked half way
between Socrates and Sir John
Falstaff'.

The last word, for the
moment, should go to the
American journalist Herman J
Mankiewicz, who asked why it
is hard to hear what a bearded
man is saying. His own answer
was: 'because he can't speak
above a whisker'.

Yours affectimately, Edward Lear.

EDWARD LEAR • 1812-1888

*Lear's self portrait, reproduced by the Royal Mail to
commemorate his centenary in 1988.*

8 *A moustache miscellany*

We did some very careful research before deciding how to divide up this book. It involved a lot of measuring of beards and moustaches and careful calculations. In the end, a ratio of seven chapters on beards to one on moustaches seemed about right. We reckon that Mr Average Beard is at least seven times hairier than Mr Average Moustache.

WELL-KNOWN MOUSTACHES

Groucho Marx first wore his false black moustache (and a frock coat) when he played the part of a schoolmaster in an act called 'Fun In Hi Skule'. He borrowed the coat from his uncle Julius, and quipped in later life: 'I tried to borrow the moustache from Uncle Julius too, but he was very proud of his moustache, and wouldn't stand still long enough for me to cut it off.'

Groucho later grew a moustache, but was told by his sister-in-law, Betty, that it did not suit him and hid his beautiful mouth. He shaved next day and went back to glueing on a false moustache for his act. This continued until the day he arrived late at the theatre

Groucho Marx (1890–1977) with his trademarks, a big cigar and a black painted-on moustache.

and had no time to paste on his phoney moustache. Instead he grabbed some black make-up and painted one on his face.

When he found that the audience laughed as much at the painted moustache, he decided to keep it. It was quicker to put on, and he no longer had the smell of the glue beneath his nose. But the manager of the theatre where he was working at the time was not pleased. 'I want the same moustache you gave 'em at the Palace,' he told Groucho. 'You

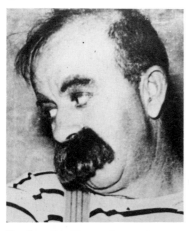

Keystone Kop Chester Conklin (1888–1971) with his distinctive false walrus.

can have it,' Groucho told him, and picked up the false moustache from his dressing table. 'Here you are—keep it.'

Another false moustache was worn by the silent-film actor/comedian Chester Conklin, born Jules Cowles (1888–1971). He used a walrus moustache as a kind of personal trademark. Like his name, the moustache was not real. He used to carry it around in his pocket so that when it was convenient for him to be recognised, he could put it on. That is a curious reversal of the normal situation. False moustaches are more usually worn by those who do not wish to be recognised.

One of the most famous moustaches in literature is that of Hercule Poirot, the dapper Belgian detective created by Agatha Christie. In an interview in *TV Times* (1989), the actor David Suchet talked of the moustache's significance to an actor who plays the part. 'The moment the moustache goes on, I take on the personality. Then, and only then, do I feel I am really Poirot. In the books the moustache is described variously. In one book it is a stiff, military moustache and in another it is small, tight and very finely curled. But the most important thing is what Poirot himself says about it. And it has to be, in his own terms, a thing of beauty. It must suit the face, because Poirot is a vain man. He has to look, in his own eyes, superb. I like the moustache. It has become my Poirot.'

The Australian cricketer Merv Hughes is known amongst other things for his Zapata-style moustache. The British journalist Andrew Duncan asked him about it in September, 1989: 'I'm happy with it. I don't have to see it, so it doesn't worry me what it looks like. I've been told it looks stupid and all sorts of things, but I've had it for five years and I'm comfortable with it, so why take it off now? People say I couldn't because it's my image—that's a crock of frogshit.'

The author Charles Dickens is another famous person who at one time wore a moustache, though we usually think of him as bearded. Writing a letter to a friend in 1844, when he would have been 32 years old, he said: 'The moustaches are glorious, glorious. I have cut them shorter and trimmed them a little at the ends to improve their shape. They are charming. Without them Life would be a blank.'

The entertainer Engelbert Humperdinck had this to say in a 1989 interview: 'You know I started the style of wearing long sideboards? And everyone followed suit. Even Elvis followed suit. But I started it. Then I shaved off my sideboards so that people would know me for my talent and not for my image. Then I grew a moustache. That started with an article in a magazine called 'America's Top Ten Sexiest Men'. I was number four in that chart and the top three all had moustaches. So I grew a moustache as well and the next year I went up to number two. So naturally, I kept the moustache.'

Dolly Sewell, a writer and broadcaster well known in her native Nottinghamshire, made some interesting points about moustaches in a local radio broadcast some time ago. Her general theme, and title of her talk, was 'I adore moustaches'. It could hardly have been otherwise. Dolly's father had a noble moustache, and one of her mother's sayings was that 'a kiss without a moustache is like apple-pie without cheese'. Dolly's husband has also had a fine moustache throughout their long marriage.

In her talk, Dolly mentioned the very thin pencilled moustache which became the trademark of the 'spiv' during World War II. She thought it was probably launched by the English actor Arthur English in one of his sketches. Dolly also recalled a music-hall song: 'It's that little bit of hair you wear upon your upper lip that tickles me, Charlie,' though this was apparently followed by the exhortation: 'Take it away!'

By the way, 'A kiss without a moustache is like an egg without salt', according to an old Spanish proverb, but Dolly's version, mentioned above, is not the only variant. Another one was mentioned by a correspondent to *The Times* newspaper in 1988. Godfrey Dodds, who wrote to say that to kiss a man with a beard, a

David Suchet and waxed moustache as Hercule Poirot.

woman needed to have the skin of a rhinoceros, gave the version: 'A kiss without a moustache is like strawberries without cream.' Alice Hutchinson prefers: 'A kiss without a moustache is like beef without mustard.'

Even great philosophers can be caught up in the 'kiss without a moustache' game. Jean-Paul Sartre, for example, comments in *Words*: 'A kiss without a moustache, they said then, is like an egg without salt. I will add to it. It is like Good without Evil.' Which presumably means that a kiss with a moustache is a combination of Good and Evil.

Mrs Katharine Acres, whose husband sports a handlebar moustache, says that he is 'a lovely kisser'. She adds: 'A girl's never been kissed properly until she's been kissed by a man with a moustache. It can get a bit dodgy when it's freezing, though. When we were courting Andre had a sports car. He's a fresh air fanatic and always had the hood down, even when the temperature was below zero. When he took me home he would try to kiss me goodnight, but I'd slam the door first. Nothing worse than being kissed by a man with a frozen moustache.'

The sexuality of the moustache is interestingly dealt with in J B Priestley's *Angel Pavement* (1930). The principal character is Mr Lena Golspie. We learn that 'his face was somewhat unusual, if only because it began by being almost bald at the top, then threw out two very bushy

eyebrows, and finally achieved a tremendous moustache, drooping a little by reason of its very length and thickness; a moustache in a thousand, with something rhetorical, even theatrical, about it'.

Later in the novel occurs the passage where Priestley delves into the subconscious mind of Miss Matfield. Talking about Golspie to Miss Morrison she describes him as brigandish. 'You ought to have him in here, so that I can meet him,' says Miss Morrison. 'But tell him to shave off that large moustache first.' 'Why should I? It doesn't matter to me. I'm not going to kiss him,' Miss Matfield added quickly, without thinking what she was saying. 'No, I suppose you're not,' said Miss Morrison meditatively. 'By the way, has he suggested you should?' (This politely avoids the question that was no doubt really in Miss Morrison's mind: 'Has it occurred to you that you should kiss him?' Perhaps she already knew the answer to that.)

A play which was staged in the 19th century, but which is unlikely to be revived, was by Robert Barnabas Brough and called *The Moustache Movement*. A typical scene had Louisa looking at Anthony's moustaches and saying, rapturously: 'Yours are such loves!' She caresses them, only to be told: 'Don't pull them about!' 'I wouldn't injure a hair of them for worlds!' says Louisa. 'They are the lodestar of my existence.' 'Louisa, I fear it is the moustaches and not the man you love,' says Anthony. 'I own it was they that won me two

Marlon Brando as the revolutionary Emiliano Zapata in the 1952 film, Viva Zapata.

months ago when we met at the Eagle,' confesses Louisa. Fortunately, she has come to love Anthony himself, for the moustaches are not real. The whole play is based upon that rather slender point.

According to Desmond Morris, in his book *Manwatching*, men sometimes twist a moustache that is not there. They are reacting, says Morris, to the passing of a beautiful girl. 'The thumb and forefinger are squeezed together in the cheek region and twisted round, as if twiddling the tip of an imaginary moustache.' Morris interprets this as a kind of male preening ritual, preceding an actual approach to the girl, or more frequently, signalling the approach that the male would like to make. He thinks it derives from the days when men, especially Italian men, had moustaches that they could actually twiddle.

A moustache makes the man, then? Yes, said the author of *Elements of Education* (1640). 'I have a favourable opinion of that young gentleman who is curious in fine mustachios. The time he employs in adjusting, dressing and curling them is no lost time; for the more he contemplates his mustachios, the more his mind will cherish and be animated by masculine and courageous notions.'

Not so sure, says Antony Horder, an Englishman who has lived and worked in France for many years. He adds that in the late 1980s moustaches were especially popular there with gay men.

MILITARY MOUSTACHES

A woman writer in 1904 said: 'The moustache, quite as much as the beard, has a wonderfully powerful effect upon a man's whole expression. The idea of virility, spirit, and manliness that it conveys is so great that it was for a long time the special privilege of officers of the army to wear it, as characteristic of the profession of arms'.

The lady was quite right, and there are many references in William Thackeray's great novel, *Vanity Fair*, to the importance of whiskers and moustaches to early 19th-century military men. We are told, for instance, that George Osborne has 'ambrosial whiskers', and that 'they had begun to do their work, and to curl themselves round the affections of Miss Swartz'.

As for mustachios, as Thackeray usually calls them, the young army officers are proud of their length and embellish them in various ways, waxing them 'into a state of brilliant polish', dyeing and scenting them. 'They walked into Mrs Osborne's drawing

room, which they perfumed with their coats and mustachios'. When the ridiculous Joseph Sedley grows a moustache, it occasions the comment: 'What the devil does a civilian mean with a moustache?'

A middle-aged man, said J Cuthbert Hadden, writing in 1893, 'can look back to the time when—male England being mostly smooth- faced—the appearance of a moustache at once declared the wearer, in the eyes of the mob, to be either a cavalry officer, an Italian fiddler, a billiard sharper, or a foreigner of some sort. It has been recorded that even in Edinburgh, most cultured and cosmopolitan of Caledonian cities, a distinguished scientist on first appearing in the streets with a moustache some 50 years ago, was followed by a rabble of rude urchins shouting 'Frenchy! Frenchy!' though he was no nearer being a Frenchman than Taffy is of being a Turk. Even in 1854, not to use the razor on the upper lip was regarded as extreme dandyism. But when the police appeared about the end of that year with their faces uncropped, the masculine world began to realise that a new era had arrived.'

NINETEENTH-CENTURY MOUSTACHES

One Victorian English gentleman who did not take too kindly to moustaches was Henry Budd. In the typical fashion of the Victorian father he made sure that his views were acted upon by his sons,

Field Marshal Horatio Herbert Kitchener (1850–1916) commanding attention with finger and moustache on a First World War recruiting poster.

even after his death. His will, made known in 1862, specified that 'in case my son Edward shall wear moustaches, the devise hereinbefore contained in favour of him, his appointees, heirs and assigns to my said estate, called Pepper Park, shall

Ronald Colman, with the popular moustache style named after him, flanked by C. Aubrey Smith and David Niven in the 1937 swashbuckling adventure film, The Prisoner of Zenda.

be void; and I devise the same estate to my son William, his appointees and heirs. And in case my son William shall wear moustaches, then the devise hereinbefore contained in favour of him, his appointees, heirs and assigns of my said estate, called Twickenham Park, shall be void; and I devise the said estate to my son Edward, his appointees and assigns.' No doubt Edward and William remained carefully clean-shaven for the rest of their lives, carefully keeping an eye on one another's upper lips.

In an article (1871) which said that clergymen could now wear beards 'without peril of the parochial Inquisition', the writer went on to say: 'Nevertheless, moustaches, we believe, are still deemed unbecoming a parson; and in all cases are generally thought to savour of dandyism.'

Social historians tell us that the moustache could be said to have well and truly come into its own for the first time in the 1890s. Until then it had been merely a subsidiary of the beard. With the decline of beards towards the end of the century, a solo moustache became not only acceptable, but almost a necessity. As the number of moustaches increased, so did the range of styles. Commentators on the period, however, say that the solo moustache did not have the cultural roots of the beard. It enjoyed only a brief spell of wide popularity, then faded soon after the start of the 20th century.

MOUSTACHES DESCRIBED

Is it possible for a moustache to be fierce, or cruel? George Bernard Shaw clearly thought so. In the stage directions of his play *Pygmalion* he says of the character Nepommuck that he 'is evidently a foreigner, guessable as a whiskered Pandour from Hungary; but in spite of the ferocity of his moustache he is amiable and genially voluble.'

Joyce Cary also describes a man with a rather dangerous sounding moustache in his *Government Baby*: 'He was a short plump man with a purple face and a curled up moustache, like two little rolls of barbed wire.'

Dylan Thomas, in *Under Milk Wood*, has a character called Mr Pugh who dreams of poisoning his wife. At one point Thomas says: 'He puts on a soft-soaping smile: it is sad and grey under his nicotine eggyellow weeping walrus Victorian moustache worn thick and long in memory of Doctor Crippen.' (The walrus moustache was actually not 'Victorian'.) The Crippen reference is to the American dentist who murdered his wife in London in 1910, dissected her body and buried it in the cellar of their home. He then sailed for America with his lover, who was disguised as a boy. The ship's captain was suspicious of Crippen's behaviour and radioed London. Crippen was arrested and subsequently executed.

In *The Story of San Michele*, Axel Munthe writes: 'The stationmaster looked up from his bundle of documents, his porcupine moustaches bristling with bewilderment.'

Damon Runyan, in *More Than Somewhat* (1937), has 'he has a moustache like a mosquito's whiskers across his upper lip.'

PROFESSIONAL MOUSTACHES

In *The Choirboys*, Joseph Wambaugh makes fun of official regulations concerning moustaches and beards. He says he is quoting from the Los Angeles Police Department manual, and that a police lieutenant took 13 weeks to compose rules such as that governing the moustache that a police officer may wear: 'A short and neatly trimmed moustache of natural color may be worn. Moustaches shall not extend below the vermilion border of the upper lip or the corners of the mouth and may not extend to the side more than one-quarter inch beyond the corners of the mouth.' This is an example of a perfect regulation, says Wambaugh, because no one can understand it.

He goes on to quote a similar ruling, slightly more confusing, about sideburns, which 'shall not extend below the bottom of the outer ear opening (the top of the earlobe) and shall end in a clean-shaven horizontal line. The flare (terminal portion of the sideburn) shall not exceed the width of the main portion of the sideburn by more than one-fourth of the unflared width'.

In 1854 a firm in Preston, Lancashire, requested that its

male employees should not wear moustaches 'during business hours'. It acknowledged, seemingly, their right to wear them in their spare time, though presumably they had to resort to false ones.

Handlebar moustaches are not especially common in Japan. When Yoshifusa Takeishi, a chauffeur who worked for the Eastern Airport Motor Company of Tokyo, grew one it did not please his employers. The moustache made Mr Takeishi look noticeably different from his fellow drivers, and in a conformist society like Japan that was not seen as a good thing. In 1979 Mr Takeishi was dismissed because he 'failed to present a pleasant image to passengers'.

Mr Takeishi took the matter to court. Two years later a Japanese judge said that it could be argued that 'wearing a moustache is not the free choice of the individual. The question can be subjected to certain restrictions set forth in the labour contracts of private firms. However,' continued the judge, 'in the plaintiff's case it was not clearly stated on the labour contract or through business practice that moustaches are prohibited'. Mr Takeishi's moustache did not have a detrimental effect on business, the judge decided, therefore the company had no right to dismiss him. He ordered the company to re-employ him.

It is unusual for a Japanese person to be so individualistic. Asked why the moustache was so important to him, Mr Takeishi said it made him look more mature. Without it he looked considerably younger than his 34 years.

George Orwell describes in his autobiographical *Down and Out in Paris and London* his days as a *plongeur* in a Paris restaurant. (In other words, he did the washing-up, 'plunging' his hands into hot water.) 'On my third day at the hotel the *chef du personnel*, who had generally spoken to me in quite a pleasant tone, called me up and said sharply:

"Here, you, shave that moustache off at once! *Nom de Dieu*, who ever heard of a *plongeur* with a moustache—nonsense! Take care I don't see you with it tomorrow."

'On the way home I asked Boris what this meant. He shrugged his shoulders. "You must do what he says, *mon ami*. No one in the hotel wears a moustache, except the cooks. I should have thought you would have noticed it. Reason? There is no reason. It is the custom."

'I saw that it was an etiquette, like not wearing a white tie with a dinner jacket, and shaved off my moustache. Afterwards I found out the explanation of the custom, which is this: waiters in good hotels do not wear moustaches, and to show their superiority they decree that *plongeurs* shall not wear them either; and the cooks wear their moustaches to show their contempt for the waiters.'

John Taylor, 'the Water poet' of the 17th century, had the following to say about moustaches in his doggerel poem *The Whip of Pride*:

> Some (spite their teeth) like
>   thatch'd eaves downward
>   grows
> And some grow upward in
>   despite their nose;
> Some their moustaches of
>   such length do keep,
> That very well they may a
>   manger sweep,
> Which in beer, ale, or wine
>   they drinking plunge,
> And suck the liquor up as
>   'twere a sponge.
> But 'tis a sloven's beastly
>   pride, I think,
> To wash his beard where
>   other men must drink.
> And some, (because they will
>   not rob the cup)
> Their upper chops like pot
>   hooks are turned up.
> The barbers thus (like tailors)
>   still must be
> Acquainted with each cut's
>   variety.

On much the same theme, the possible disadvantages of a long moustache, another 17th-century writer had this to say: 'Although we endeavour to prevent these Mustacho-haires while we eat, yet they descend, and entering together with the meat into the mouth are bitten with the teeth, whose peeces we are compelled either to spit out, or sometimes imprudently to devour: and if we drink, these haires swim in our drinke, moystened with whose sprinkling dew they drop down upon the beard of the Chin and Cloaths, which is an unseemly sight.' The same writer added that a long moustache is a hindrance to spitting, and made

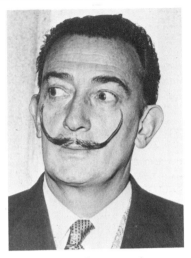

Once seen, never forgotten — the Mephistopheles moustache of Salvador Dali (1904–89).

it difficult to speak clearly. He also thought that the weight of a heavy moustache might distort the upper lip.

The moustache 'sops itself full of soup and gravy and coffee and is absurd besides,' said the writer of a magazine article in 1904. 'It is grown purely for vanity, with the hope of adding a certain fierceness to the innate sheepishness of the wearer's expression.' The same writer was not much in favour of beards. 'To be perfectly frank, at the risk of being somewhat disgusting, we must own that the full beard collects dandruff, which plentifully bestrews the neckcloth and the waistcoat.'

The late John Roy would not have been impressed by nasty comments about long moustaches. His own handlebar moustache was seen by many millions of people, thanks to his countless television

*Current UK 'longest moustache' champion Edward Sedman, whose 'wing span' is
129 cm 51 in — seen here on Sky Television's* Jameson Tonight *programme.*

John Roy's 189 cm 74.5 in handlebar.

appearances. At its longest it measured 189 cm *74.5 in,* from tip to tip, making him the British record-holder. (The current UK champion is Edward Sedman, whose moustache runs to 129 cm *51 in.* This pales into insignificance when compared with that of Birger Pellas of Sweden, who began growing his moustache in 1973. By 3 February, 1989 it had reached a length of 286 cm *9 ft 4.5 in.*) Mr Roy, aged 76 when he was interviewed in 1986 by Alasdair Riley, said 'Aye, the lassies love it. They cannae keep their hands off me. I've kissed girls all over the world and they'll be kissing me before they close the lid when the day of reckoning comes. And sure as hell, my moustache will make a nice wee bonfire when I arrive down below. The devil himself will want to kiss me before I'm consigned to the flames.'

Masuriya Din of India sporting his 258 cm 8 ft 6 in long moustache.

Mr Roy was for 20 years president of the Handlebar Club, which meets in a London pub on the first Friday of each month. The club was formed in his dressing room at the Windmill Theatre by the British comedian Jimmy Edwards in April 1947. Membership reached a peak in the 1950s, when 250 mainly ex-service members gathered to admire one another's moustaches. In recent years membership has fallen dramatically as long moustaches become less fashionable.

John Roy was not one to care much about the prevailing fashion. A Japanese television producer who offered him £2000 to have his moustache cut off during a live television transmission was told in no uncertain terms what he could do with the money.

Nicholas Bentley would presumably have accepted the money. His comment, made in the 1950s, was that some men 'having no other attribute worthy of interest, now feel they must claim attention by the size and unruly behaviour of their moustaches'. Bentley preferred what he called 'good, honest, work-a-day' moustaches, though he suggested that they be left untrimmed so that they become 'a useful aid against minestrone'.

Some useful advice for anyone thinking of growing a moustache comes from a book on etiquette published in 1904. All depends on the size of the nose that will accompany it. 'A man with a trivial nose should

Douglas Fairbanks Jr with a pencil line moustache.

not wear a large moustache. Doing so will increase the insignificance of his insignificant nose. With a large nose, the moustache may be large too, but its ends should never extend further than in a straight line with the outer corners of the eyes. Sometimes the ends of a man's moustache are visible to persons walking behind him. This imparts to him a belligerent, aggressive air that makes small children refrain from asking him the time.'

A Handbook of Etiquette, published in 1859, had this to say: 'The moustache should be neat and not too large, and such fopperies as cutting the points thereof or twisting them up to the fineness of needles — though patronized by the Emperor of the French — are decidedly a proof of vanity.'

The very thin narrow moustache which covers the full

width of the upper lip, with shaven skin above and below it, is usually associated with the American actor Douglas Fairbanks. The first man to wear it, however, was probably Charles II, who introduced this fashion when he was restored to the English throne in 1660.

The toothbrush moustache, according to John Brophy in his book *The Human Face*, became popular amongst British soldiers in World War I. The name derived from the narrow oblong shape of the moustache, with the bristles being cut short. Brophy says the moustache was practical at the time because of the unhygienic conditions which prevailed in the trenches. Water for washing was sometimes unobtainable for weeks on end. Men were obliged to crop their heads and keep facial hair to a minimum in order to avoid being lice-ridden.

In Chinese operas, villains, inn-keepers and low-class characters are often portrayed with toothbrush moustaches. A pencil-line moustache denotes a rich playboy type who takes advantage of others and is not to be trusted. Warriors are likely to have bushy beards, while long beards are given to the very wise or the very old. The Fu Manchu style of moustache is more Hollywood fiction than Chinese fact.

England, at the beginning of the 1970s, was 'the hairiest England since Regency times', according to Morris Lurie, writing in the *Telegraph Magazine* in 1972. Bearded postmen were two a penny, said Lurie, and on all sides were 'devilishly wicked Mongolian moustaches, bushy mutton chops, Mississippi riverboat sideburns, beehive Afros and shoulder-length tresses'.

In the same article, *Keeping a Cool Head*, Lurie reported on his investigation of various fashionable London barber shops. At G F Trumper's he was shown the tongs used for curling moustaches, still occasionally in demand.

AMERICAN MOUSTACHES

The US and Britain have occasionally been out of step in the matter of beards and moustaches. A correspondent to the *Daily Telegraph* in 1986, Henry G Button of Cambridge, mentioned the example of Frank Woolworth, of the department store family. When Woolworth first came to Britain in the early years of the 20th century, he was clean-shaven in the American fashion. He saw that a moustache was needed in England to give him the

Charles II (1630–85) with a pencil line.

necessary air of authority so immediately began to grow one. Subsequently he would shave when he boarded the liner to take him back to the States, and start growing his moustache when he embarked for England.

American presidents have not been noted for their moustaches. Only three have sported them, Presidents Cleveland, Roosevelt and Taft.

Dr A A Brill, an American psycho-analyst, was of the opinion in the 1940s that because the stereotyped image of the ideal American was a clean-cut, clean-shaven youth, men tended to shave their moustaches as they got older. They were trying to wipe out the signs of age by doing so, he suggested, though they may have grown the moustaches in the first place in order to look older.

American barbers in the 1940s are reported to have declared that men with moustaches 'are fussy as old maids, very difficult to please'.

(Perhaps one thing moustache wearers ought to be fussy about is whether they talk about a moustache or moustaches. These days we tend to say a moustache, even when a man wears two separate moustaches, divided by a clean-shaven area beneath the nose.
'And he twirl'd his moustache
  with so charming an air
—His moustaches, I should say,
  because he'd a pair.'

Three presidential moustaches — Grover Cleveland (1837–1908), Theodore 'Teddy' Roosevelt (1858–1919) and William Howard Taft (1857–1930).

GALLERY OF MOUSTACHES
NOT INCLUDED ELSEWHERE

Adolphe Menjou

Box car

Bullet heads

Chevron

Horseshoe

Howie

Major

Mistletoe

Painter's brush

Pyramidal

Regent

Shermanic

Strip-Teaser

This verse from *The Black Mousquetaire*, in Barham's *Ingoldsby Legends*, seems to indicate that whichever form was used in writing, the pronunciation, imitating the French, remained the same.)

Perhaps because the problems of long moustaches in acting as soup-strainers had become generally recognized, it became customary at the turn of the century to crop them fairly closely. American barbers at the time asked their customers if they wanted their moustaches 'stubbed'.

MOUSTACHE CRITICS

Edith Effron, writing in the *New York Times Magazine* in 1944, said of the moustache: 'it plays many roles today — South American suavity, French affectation, Sicilian villainy. It is Chaplin-pathetic, Hitler-

The 'little tramp' with the toothbrush moustache.

psychopathic, Gable-debonair, Lou Lehr-wacky. It perplexes. It fascinates. It amuses. And it repels.'

An Australian psychiatrist, N Parker, had this to say in 1969: 'Gentlemen who wear

Adolf Hitler (1889–1945) wearing a toothbrush.

moustaches are generally obsessive, psychopathic, impotent or have some other sexual problem.' This seems a pretty wide-ranging statement until you think about it. Parker was obviously thinking only of Australians, and more particularly, of Australian 'gentlemen'. Rumour has it that no one has been able to work out who exactly he had in mind, since no Australian with a moustache will ever admit to being a gentleman.

OUTSIDE HELP

The American *Barbers' Journal* in 1902 carried an advertisement for the Kaiser Mustache Trainer. The inclusion of the word 'Kaiser' would have reminded potential customers of a moustache which was at that time known throughout the western world, borne by Kaiser Wilhelm II of Germany. The product being advertised was said to have a 'patented flexible comb attachment, which will train the moustache to any desired shape without inconvenience'. Wearing it for five minutes a day after washing the face, said the advertising blurb, would shape the moustache for the day. Wearing it all night a few times would have a permanent effect, shaping the moustache for all time. The main purpose of the trainer was to cause the moustache to turn upwards, so that it no longer stained the coat front by drooping on it. Customers could rid themselves of this particular kind of masculine droop by investing 50 cents in the gadget, which is said to have worked quite well.

In the 19th century it was thought that onion juice would help to thicken up a moustache. In *Wrinkles and Notions for Every Household* (1890), Mrs de Salis also offered this recipe for hirsute happiness: 'Take 1 oz of tincture of cantharides, the same of tincture of capiscum and 1 oz of rosewater to make a lotion, which rub into the moustache morning and night.' This may not have caused the moustache to grow more quickly, but at least it would have made it smell sweeter.

The moustache, according to the 19th-century writer Edwin Chadwick, 'is a natural respirator, defending the lungs from the inhalation of dust and cold. Not only that: it is helpful in preventing toothache, colds, bronchitis and mumps.'

Kaiser Wilhelm II of Germany (1859–1941).

LOVE THY MOUSTACHE

The English writer and artist John Leighton, co-founder of the Royal Photographic Society, was arrested in London at the age of 65, charged with being in a public thoroughfare dressed in female attire.

A press report of the time minutely described his outfit, which included a blue serge shirt fringed with red, a black jersey-like bodice, a light-coloured cape with a Medici collar, unusually large high-heeled shoes and a dark green matador hat. All very tasteful, but Mr Leighton was also wearing a bristly grey moustache. It was this which had aroused the suspicions of passers-by.

Mr Leighton claimed that he was doing research for a book he intended to write about women's clothes. He should perhaps have written one about moustaches. It is clear that he loved his own effort. He was obviously prepared to go to great lengths to get his facts right about feminine attire, but he could not sacrifice those bristles on his upper lip. He deserves his place in the moustache-lovers' Hall of Fame.

9 Words bewhiskered

To end with, on a slightly more serious note, here is a beard, moustache and whiskers word-list. It is derived from the works of the main writers on such matters since the 17th century. They include Richard Corson, author of *Fashions in Hair*; J Stevens Cox, FSA, author of *An Illustrated Dictionary of Hairdressing and Wigmaking*; J A Dulaure, whose *Pogonologia* was translated from the French in 1786; G A Foan, editor of *The Art and Craft of Hairdressing*; T S Gowing, author of *The Philosophy of Beards*; S Trusty, author of *The Art and Science of Barbering*; Reginald Reynolds, whose *Beards*, published in 1950, is certainly the most comprehensive literary survey of the subject. It strangely restricts itself to words, though, where some illustrations would have greatly helped.

We have of course consulted many other works, including various dictionaries of British and American slang. They record how beards and moustaches have been described in everyday speech. Unfortunately, there is no such thing as a definitive list of words for the different styles of beards, moustaches and whiskers. Writers of the past have tended to attach labels which were meaningful to them and their immediate audience, but which have become obscure with the passing of time. A 17th-century writer, for instance, would happily describe a beard as a sugar-loaf and be certain that readers would immediately visualize the shape he had in mind. An Englishman writing soon after World War I could describe moustache styles in terms of the soldiers who typically wore them, but for later generations descriptions such as general, major and the like mean rather little.

We have tried to record those terms which gained some kind of general currency, and those which are intrinsically interesting. Just as an apple becomes more specifically a Cox's, a Granny Smith, an Alice or a Pretty Maid to a specialist, so a beard, moustache or set of whiskers becomes an imperial, toothbrush and Dundrearies to a pogonologist. Words like pogonologist, by the way, are included in our list. You could say that he (or she) is a person who, when calling a spade a spade, knows exactly what kind of beard is meant.

Abraham or Abram beard: this is not, as it happens, a reference to the beard of the Hebrew patriarch. Abraham or Abram is here a corruption of the word 'auburn'. References to 'Abraham-coloured beards' occur in late 16th-, early 17th-century texts.

Adolphe Menjou: a style of moustache made well known by the French-American leading man of the 1920s, known as Hollywood's best-dressed man. Menjou appeared in his first film in 1916. He was last seen in *Pollyanna*, released in 1960. (See page 111.)

Airedales: in early cinema slang, a name for bearded actors, referring to Airedale terriers.

Algernon: any man who sports whiskers or a moustache could correctly be addressed as Algernon. The name derives from Norman French *als gernons*, 'with whiskers or moustaches'. Most Normans, as the Bayeux tapestry reveals, were clean-shaven, so that a man with a hairy face was highly likely to attract a nickname.

Algernon has never been especially popular as a first name. Its cause was probably not helped by Oscar Wilde, who has a character of the name in *The Importance of Being Earnest* say: 'I really can't see why you should object to the name of Algernon. It is not at all a bad name. In fact, it is rather an aristocratic name. Half of the chaps who go into the Bankruptcy Court are called Algernon.'

Anchor: a beard style roughly resembling an anchor. (See page 41.)

Artillery whiskers: another name for Dundrearies, which were especially associated in the 19th century with Artillery officers. (See page 40.)

Assyrian beard: a long beard dressed in spiral curls or plaits. (See page 64.)

Aureole beard: the aureole is the golden circle of light, the halo, that surrounds the head of a saint or martyr in religious paintings. The word has been used to describe a rounded beard, a kind of hairy halo beneath the chin.

Awn: the term used by botanists to describe the delicate spines on the end of the barley grain-sheath; commonly called the 'beard' of the barley.

Balbo: a short chin beard of the style worn by Italo Balbo (1896–1940), the Italian aviator and politician. (See page 40.)

Bald face: in the 19th-century dialect of Somerset, this was the term for a man without whiskers.

Barb: sometimes used in 15th-century English for the beard. It is based on Latin *barba*, 'beard'. Later the verb to barb meant to shave someone.

Barbal: of or belonging to a beard.

Barbated: in zoology and botany, 'bearded'.

Barbatulous: having only a small beard.

Barber: now more usually a hairdresser, but originally a trimmer of beards.

Barbula: 'little beard'. Sometimes used specifically of the *pique-devant* style, a tiny tuft of hair under the middle of the lower lip.

Bard: the surname Bard has at least six different possible origins. As a Jewish family name it is likely to be from German Bart or Yiddish bord, both of which mean 'beard'. If so it would have been a nickname originally for a man with an especially luxuriant beard. The Scottish name Baird looks as if it should be connected with beard, but it comes from either a place name or refers to a minstrel, a bard.

Beard:
● the family name Beard usually refers to an ancestor who was bearded at the time when most men were clean-shaven, or whose beard was particularly worthy of note because of its length, colour or thickness. The surname can also derive from an English place name, indicating where the family were living centuries ago.
● black American slang for an intellectual person, according to Clarence Major in his *Black Slang*.
● British readers might be slightly bewildered by this passage in *The Storyteller*, by Harold Robbins: 'AJ's invited me to dinner at Perino's with his banker.' 'Just the three of you?' 'AJ's wife and a starlet the banker has the hots for.' 'Where do you fit in?' 'I'm the beard.'

This is a use of an American slang term from the world of gambling, where a 'beard' is an agent, used to conceal the identity of the principal. In this case the first speaker has been invited along to lunch as the supposed partner of the starlet, although she will really be with the banker.

Beard someone (Beard the lion in his den): to face someone boldly in his own territory, especially someone superior, e.g. the boss in his own office.

Beardie:
● a general nickname for a bearded person. In the 1960s, especially, journalists were likely to talk of beardy-weirdies.
● an Australian nickname for the followers of John Wroe, who founded a sect called the Christian Israelites. *The Daily Chronicle* reported in 1905: 'There is only one founder of a religion buried in Australia — John Wroe, who started the Christian Israelites, nicknamed the Beardies, since they never cut their hair.'
● a common name for the bearded collie, a kind of sheepdog with long hair.

Beardlet: occasionally used to describe a small beard. Belloc, writing of Cardinal Richelieu, mentions 'the military moustache and beardlet of that pointed face'.

Beardman: *The Dictionary of Jamaican English* by Cassidy and Le Page defines this expression as 'an adherent of the Rastafarian cult; specifically, one who wears a beard and plentiful hair, but trims them at times.' A beardman contrasts with a locksman, whose hair is matted and plaited and never cut.

Beard-splitter: late 17th- and early 18th-century slang for a man who frequented brothels or was a womanizer.

Beaver: slang word for a beard and the name of a game which was popular in the 1920s. (More at page 83.)

Billies: full medium-length chin whiskers also called Billy whiskers.

Bodkin: a beard style of the 17th century, resembling the short dagger known as a bodkin. (See pages 40, 67.)

Box car: a rarely-used moustache style, named for its resemblance to a box car freight wagon. (See page 111.)

Breakwater: a short goatee beard. (See page 41.) The longer goatee was called an Uncle Sam.

Bullet heads: a style of moustache curled at each end near the corners of the mouth. (See page 111.)

Burnsides: a style of mutton-chop whiskers plus moustache, as worn by General Ambrose Burnside. The original form of Sideburns. (See page 84.)

Bush: a slang word for any beard, especially a bushy one. (See pages 17, 41.)

Cads: this is thought to have referred to the kind of beard popular in Cadiz, Spain, in the 17th century. References to a cads beard appear far too early to mean the kind of beard worn by a cad in the modern sense of the word.

Captain Kettle set: a reference to the full set of beard and moustache worn by Captain Owen Kettle, a fictional seafaring hero created by C J Cutliffe Hyne. The stories relating the adventures of this merchant navy skipper began to appear in book form in 1897. Some low-budget films were made later. (See page 75.)

Cathedral: a long, full beard of the kind formerly associated with high-ranking ecclesiastics. (See page 41.)

Charley, Charlie: the name of a small triangular beard, as worn by Charles I. Also used of a moustache, as worn by the actor/comedian Charles Chaplin. (See pages 48, 112.)

Chevron: a moustache shaped roughly like a chevron, the stripe used to distinguish non-commissioned officers. (See page 111.)

Chin-beard: a term used by R L Stevenson in *St Ives*: 'The speaker wore a chin-beard of considerable length, and the remainder of his face was blue with shaving.' Elsewhere in the novel is a reference to 'a chin-beard in the American fashion'. Presumably a long goatee is meant, an Uncle Sam. (See pages 8, 40.)

Chin curtain: an American name for a narrow band of whiskers around the face and chin.

Colman: a moustache style made well known by the

British-born film actor Ronald Colman (1891–1958). (See page 102.)

Consort: a moustache style trimmed to the width of the mouth and with a central parting.

Ducktail: a rare beard style with the hair brushed towards the centre. (See page 41.)

Dundrearies: long flowing side-whiskers, separated by a clean-shaven chin. Also known as 'Piccadilly weepers'. Lord Dundreary is an aristocratic idiot in a play by Tom Taylor, *Our American Cousin* (1858). Incidentally, President Lincoln was watching the play the night he was assassinated in a Washington theatre in 1865. The part of Lord Dundreary was created by an Englishman, E A Sothern. His adoption of the side-whiskers for the role was no doubt meant to add to the character's general silliness, but many 19th-century men found such whiskers to their liking. Many references to Dundrearies (or Dundrearys) are found in literature. F Anstey, in *Vice Versa* (1882), refers to 'bushy black whiskers, more like the antiquated Dundreary type than modern fashion permits'. C G Harper, in *Revolted Woman* (1894) has: 'This fashion was the "Piccadilly weeper" variety of adornment, known at this day — chiefly owing to Sothern's impersonation of a contemporary lisping fop — as the "Dundreary".' In his *Man of Property* (1906) John Galsworthy writes: 'His cheeks, thinned by two parallel folds, were framed within Dundreary whiskers.' *The Bridge of Life* (1929), by C H Smith, has: 'The older men wore beards, Dundrearys or side-whiskers; the middle-aged mustaches.' (See page 40.)

Eleven-a-side: a name given to a very small, under-the-nose moustache, supposedly referring to the number of hairs it contains.

Face fittings: Australian slang for a moustache, or beard, or both.

Face fungus: a colloquial term for whiskers, beard or moustache.

Face lace (also Lacé curtains): listed in *American Tramp and Underworld Slang*, by Godfrey Irwin, as terms for whiskers.

Forked: Chaucer's merchant in *The Canterbury Tales* had a forked beard. This style was especially popular in the 14th century. The beard was shaped with the hand rather than cut, according to a French barber writing on the subject. The object was to produce two peaks instead of the usual single peak. Fork-beard or forked-beard is also the name given to various species of fish. (See pages 40, 59.)

Franz Josef: a beard style named after that worn by the Austrian Emperor, Franz Josef (1830–1916).

Full (also full set): facial hair allowed to grow unchecked as whiskers, moustache and beard. (See pages 12, 27, 72, 73, 91.)

Goatee: a small tufted beard

hanging from the centre of the chin, named for its resemblance to the beard of a he-goat. In the 19th century it was thought to be a typically American beard, judging by the remarks of an Englishwoman who was travelling in the US in the 1850s: 'They [Americans] also indulge in eccentricities of appearance in the shape of beards and imperials, not to speak of the "goatee".' Goats-beard is a name applied to several plants, such as meadowsweet and salsify. (See page 40.)

Hairy Bob: Yorkshire dialect for a bearded man.

Half: a style whereby one side of the chin is shaven, while the other is bearded. A style said to have been favoured by the American Indians of Virginia in the 16th and 17th centuries. (See page 22.)

Hammer cut: a style of beard and moustache in which the narrow beard resembles the handle of a hammer, and the moustache its head. In the 17th century known as a Roman T. (See page 40.)

Handlebar: a moustache style where the ends protrude from the side of the face, thus suggesting the handlebars on a bicycle. The style was very popular during World War II with officers of the Royal Air Force. (See pages 106, 110.)

Hirsute: an adjective often used as a synonym for 'hairy'. It more properly describes hair which is shaggy and untrimmed. Hirsuto- can be

used to form learned words such as hirsuto-atrous, 'with black hair', hirsuto-rufous, 'with red hair', etc.

Hispid: an adjective meaning 'having rough hair or bristles'. The associated noun is hispidity. Try asking a man what reason lies behind his hispidity — is he trying to grow a beard or did he merely forget to shave?

Hold-all: slang for a bushy beard.

Hollywoodian: a moustache and beard style covering the lower half of the face only, the sideboards and chin immediately below the lower lip being clean-shaven. (See page 40.)

Horace Greeley: a late 19th-century American beard-cut, comprising a fringe of whiskers under the chin. Named after the editor of the *New York Tribune* during the Civil War.

Horseshoe: a moustache that hangs over each corner of the mouth and reaches below the chin. (See page 111.)

Howie: a style of moustache, that tapers towards turned-up ends. (See page 111.)

Imperial: a small beard, little more than a tuft of hair, growing beneath the centre of the lower lip. It was made fashionable by Napoleon III circa 1840 and was named in his honour, though it had been worn by others previously. (See page 71.)

Kaiser: a moustache with turned-up ends, as worn by

Wilhelm II of Germany. (See page 113.)

Lace curtains: See Face lace.

Ladykillers: an occasional synonym for Dundrearies. (See page 40.)

Lavatory brush: Royal Naval slang for the cut of beard favoured by submariners during World War II.

Lee boards: Royal Navy slang for side-whiskers.

Lincolnic: a beard-cut named after the US President, Abraham Lincoln. (See page 72.)

Lip fuzz: American slang for a moustache of any kind.

Lip tickler: slang for a moustache. Also known occasionally as lip spinach, lip puff.

Major, the: an English moustache style supposedly favoured by Army majors. Similarly, a number of other moustaches were named after military personnel, among them the Captain, the General, the Guardsman, the Sergeant-Major. (See page 111.)

Marquisotte: this word appears in various forms in the late 16th century, e.g. *marquisette*, Marquis Otto. It was borrowed from French, and was defined by a contemporary writer as 'a beard cut after the Turkish fashion, all being shaven away but the mustachioes'. The verb was sometimes used passively, to say that a man had been marquisotted. Later writers sometimes applied the name marquisotte to any small well-trimmed beard.

Masonic beard: an occasional term for a fan-shaped beard, thought to be a style favoured by freemasons.

Meat axe: a humorous description of a beard shaped like a meat-axe, with a wide, straight bottom.

Medium full: a full set of whiskers, moustache and beard, but with the latter trimmed close to the chin. (See page 41.)

Mephistopheles: a name for the long, waxed moustache that projects beyond the corners of the mouth and then turns upwards towards the ears. The devil of this name who appears in Goethe's *Faust* and several 17th-century English dramas is often portrayed with such a moustache. Mephistopheles is bad Greek for 'one who dislikes light'. Also the name of a medium-long, sharp-pointed beard, as often worn in stage productions by actors playing this devil. (See page 105.)

Mexican: a thin, drooping moustache which is dressed along the upper lip but does not cover it. The ends are turned down on either side of the mouth.

Milk-chopped: a reference to someone whose 'chops', or cheeks, are clean-shaven.

Miner's: a straight or slightly fan-shaped beard (wider at the bottom than the top) of reasonable length, characterized by being cut off squarely at the bottom. (See page 41.)

Misopogon, or **misopogonist:** someone who hates beards.

Misplaced eyebrow: a humorous reference to a small moustache.

Mistletoe: a moustache style thought to resemble mistletoe leaves. (See page 111.)

Mouse-tail: a slang expression for a very thin moustache.

Moustache: this is the usual modern British spelling of the word, taken from the French. Earlier English dictionaries, such as that of Johnson, prefer mustache, as do all modern American dictionaries. The word derives from Italian *mostaccio*, which means snout as well as moustache. It was earlier written mustachio in English (though in many variant spellings). It is thought to be connected ultimately with a dialectal Greek word meaning mouth or jaws, though when it was first introduced into English in the 16th century many writers seem to have associated it with Spanish *muchacho*, 'boy'.

Moustache lifter: a device used by the Ainus of Japan, who are noted for their hairiness. It is said to be shaped like a paper-knife, and is designed to keep the moustache away from any liquid when a man is drinking.

Moustache guard and trainer: over the years moustachioed men have used a variety of protective devices, including the moustache guard—a band of cloth, soft leather, or even metal, which was secured around the head with elastic or strings during meal times (see page 114). Similar protection was sometimes worn at night to retain an upward curl. Another such device, the moustache trainer or 'Schnurrbartbinde', was much favoured in Germany by army officers during the time of Kaiser Wilhelm II.

Mouth-stache (also mout-stash): forms of the word moustache used in Jamaica.

Mush brush: a bushy moustache. 'Mush', or 'moosh', is a slang word referring to the face, though the origin of the expression is unknown. No one seems to have suggested that it might derive from moustache.

Mustachios (or Mustaches): a slang term in Prohibition days (1920–33) for high-ranking members of the Mafia, even though they might be clean-shaven. First-generation Mafiosi in the US all wore handlebar moustaches.

Mutton chops: side-whiskers trimmed roughly to the shape of mutton chops, narrow at the top but broad and rounded at the bottom. (See page 41.)

Muzzle: a mainly 18th-century slang expression for a long, straggly and perhaps dirty beard. The word correctly applies to the front part of an animal's face. It was jokingly applied to the human face, especially the nose, mouth and chin, then extended to refer to the beard.

Mystax: used by the entomologists to describe the line of hairs above the mouth in e.g. the common house-fly.

Napoleon III: another name for the Imperial beard, worn by Napoleon III. (See page 71.)

Natural bush: this has been used to describe a beard which is never cut or trimmed in any way, but is left to grow as it will. The humorous writer Frank Richardson also refers to a beard as 'natural ivy'.

Needle: a long, finely pointed beard style of the 16th and 17th centuries. (See page 40.)

Neptunian: a three-pointed forked beard, supposedly resembling the trident that the sea-god Neptune is usually depicted as carrying.

Newgate collar (also known as the Tyburn collar): a 19th-century British slang term for a beard worn around the chin like a collar, or more specifically, like a hangman's rope. Newgate was a famous London prison, finally demolished in 1902. Its name came to mean 'prison' as a general term. This type of beard was also known grimly as a Newgate frill or fringe.

Newgate ring: 19th-century slang for a moustache and beard worn as one, without side-whiskers. (See Newgate collar.)

Nose clip moustache: an artificial moustache, held in position against the upper lip by means of a clip fixed to the central wall of the nostrils.

Old Bill: an occasional synonym for a walrus moustache.

Old Dutch: a beard style which is trimmed to give a square look to the face, the hair above and below the mouth being removed. (See page 40.)

Old moustache: 19th-century slang for an old soldier.

Olympian: used to describe a very long, full beard, of the type associated with the Greek gods of Mount Olympus, especially Zeus. Often referred to as a flowing or patriarchal beard. (See page 40.)

Painter's brush: a moustache style vaguely resembling a wide painter's brush. (See page 111.)

Parted: a beard which has a central parting, each side being combed or brushed separately. The style is said to make a narrow face look broader. (See page 40.)

Pencil: a narrow strip of beard from the lower lip to the chin.

Pencil line: commonly used to describe a very thin moustache. It can be a real one, or drawn on the upper lip by a coloured cosmetic. (See pages 108, 109.)

Piccadilly weepers: applied especially to Dundreary side-whiskers when the latter extended below the chin. They were so called because they were much favoured by the elegant gentlemen who paraded themselves in London's Piccadilly area in the 1850s and 60s. (See page 40.)

Pilosity: hairiness, especially when the hairs are not too bushy.

Pique-devant: another name for a short, pointed beard. The style, fashionable in France in the 16th and 17th centuries, was also known in English as pick-a-devant. (See page 67.)

Pisa: the Pisa beard, referred to

for instance by Beaumont and Fletcher in *The Queen of Corinth*, seems to have been the same as a stiletto beard. (See pages 64, 67.)

pogon: the Greek word for 'beard' gives rise to a number of English words, such as

pogoniasis — an excessive growth of hair on a person, e.g. a beard which grows on a woman
pogoniate — bearded
pogonic — pertaining to the beard
pogonolatry — the practice of swearing by the beard. 'By my beard' was an Elizabethan oath, found in Shakespeare and other 17th-century playwrights.
pogonologist — a serious student of beards, a writer on beards
pogonology (or *pogonologia*) — the scientific study of the beard
pogonophile — an admirer or lover of beards
pogonophobia — an abnormal dislike or fear of beards
pogonotomist — a trimmer of beards, a shaver, a barber
pogonotomy — beard-cutting or shaving. This was used as the title of a book by the Frenchman Jean-Jacques Perret in 1771. Perret was a forerunner of King Gillette, and inventor of a crude safety razor.
pogonotrophist — someone who grows a beard
pogonotrophy — the growing and cultivation of a beard. Constantine IV, Emperor of Rome, was called Pogonatus, the Bearded.

To these one may add
misopogonist — hater of beards
philopogonist — another term for a lover of beards

Polar beaver: Frank Richardson's humorous term for a man with a full white beard, or 'cotton wool beaverage'.

Pyramidal: a moustache style vaguely recalling the shape of a pyramid. (See page 111.)

Quadrate: a term used in the 16th and 17th centuries to describe a square-shaped beard.

Regent: an early 20th-century moustache style. (See page 111.)

Rimmers: a 19th-century American narrow beard running around the chin-line. (See page 40.)

Roman T: a short, straight moustache worn with a long, narrow beard. 'The Roman T. Your T beard is the fashion,' says a character in *The Queen of Corinth* (1647), by Beaumont and Fletcher. Other contemporary writers use the term. A modern synonym is hammer cut. (See page 40.)

Round: a bushy beard with a round outline. (See pages 41, 62.)

Royale: an occasional synonym for an imperial beard. (See page 71.)

Saucer: a narrow beard running beneath the chin line. Also known as a trencher beard. (See page 29.)

Screw: this beard style was found in the 17th century. It consisted of a narrow, twisted tuft of beard, extending from the lower lip to one or two inches beyond the chin. (See page 77.)

Scurze: Royal Naval slang for a bearded man, though the word derives from whi-skers.

Shadow: a young, thin moustache.

Shenandoah: an occasional synonym in the US for the spade beard. The allusion is to beards worn by soldiers fighting in the American Civil War. The Shenandoah Valley, in western Virginia, was the site of much military activity in the 1860s. (See page 41.)

Shermanic: a moustache style named after the American general William Tecumseh Sherman (1820–91), who captured Atlanta in the Civil War and forced the Confederate army northwards. (See page 111.)

Shrubbery: applied colloquially to either a natural or false beard.

Sidebars, Sideboards, Side-whiskers: all three terms appeared at the end of the 19th century to describe the whiskers which grow at the side of the face, in front of the ears. The first term is now obsolete. Eric Partridge tells us in his *Dictionary of Historical Slang* that the word sideboards was first applied to a shirt collar with starched wings. That may have suggested its later use for whiskers. (See page 87.)

Sideburns: it is generally accepted that this word was coined by adapting the name of General Ambrose Burnside

(1824–81), a Union general in the Civil War. The general wore side-whiskers which joined up with a full moustache. He was otherwise clean-shaven. (See page 84.)

Side-whiskers: See sidebars.

Sidies: colloquially used for side-whiskers.

Sloping box car: a variation of the box car moustache with the ends slanting down.

Son-of-a-bitch: Australian slang in the 1890s for the moustache and imperial beard favoured by cattle-buyers and wool inspectors.

Soup strainer: a popular name for a full moustache, tending to droop over the mouth, a walrus. (See pages 96, 110.)

Spade: there are many references in 17th-century literature to the spade beard, or spade peak as it was also called, but it is not clear exactly which shape is meant. Spades could be broad-bladed, with a slightly rounded edge, or almost pointed. It has even been suggested that 'spade' when applied to a beard was a reference to the more rounded playing-card symbol rather than the tool, though the *Oxford English Dictionary* does not support this view. (See page 41.)

Spinach: an American slang term for a beard.

Square button: See Toothbrush.

Square-cut: a general term for any beard which is cut squarely at the end. (See page 40.)

Stash: slang for a moustache.

Stiletto: this short dagger with a relatively thick blade was introduced to England from Italy at the beginning of the 17th century. The word was quickly applied to a short pointed beard resembling the weapon. The Earl of Southampton was amongst those who wore it. (See page 67.)

Strip-teaser: an American moustache cut very narrow with the ends curving up slightly. (See page 111.)

Stubble beard: used of a very short, spiky beard covering the whole of the hair-growing area on the face. (See pages 10, 11.)

Sugar loaf: a conical beard resembling the shape of a sugar loaf. (See page 41.)

Swallow tail: a long, forked beard shaped like a swallow tail. (See page 41.)

Tash: slang for a moustache.

Tickler: variant of lip-tickler.

Tile: another name for the miner's beard. (See page 41.)

Toothbrush: a small, square, bristly moustache of the type worn by Adolf Hitler. Also known as a square button or Charlie Chaplin. (See page 112.)

Toshy: a nickname in Yorkshire dialect for a hairy-faced man, according to Julian Franklyn in *A Dictionary of Nicknames*. He says that the same word applied to a woman means that she is over-dressed.

Trencher beard: See Saucer. (See page 29.)

Tuft: occasionally used as a synonym for a beard, especially a goatee or an imperial.

Tyburn collar: 19th-century English slang for a fringe of beard worn under the chin. The allusion is to the hangman's rope.

Uncle Sam: a name given at one time to a long goatee. It contrasted with the short version, which was known as a Breakwater. (See page 40.)

Vandyke: a pointed beard worn with a waxed moustache but without side-whiskers. It takes its name from the Flemish painter Sir Anthony Van Dyke or Van Dyck (1599–1641), known mostly for his portraits and religious paintings. Many of the men whose portraits he painted, including Charles I, wore beards and moustaches of the kind described above. (See pages 47, 48.)

Walrus: a large moustache which overhangs the lips, resembling that of a walrus. T Fitzgibbon has written: 'I remember Conan Doyle as a large man with sad thoughtful eyes and a walrus moustache.' In American slang of the 1920s a walrus was a fat person. (See pages 96, 110.)

Waxed: any moustache that has been dressed with wax, usually with both ends pointed. (See page 97.)

Weepers: See Piccadilly weepers. (See page 40.)

Whisker: in English slang of the

17th and 18th centuries, a lie, especially a 'whopper'. Later the colloquial retort to a highly improbable story was 'the mother of that was a whisker'. In more modern American radio slang, applied to a verbal blunder while broadcasting, a fluff. The word whisker is connected with the verb to whisk, in the sense of whisking, or brushing, something away. It was jokingly applied to the hair on a man's face because it resembled a kind of brush.

Whiskerade: a fine display of whiskers.

Whiskerando: a jocular 19th-century word for a man with bushy whiskers. There is a character in Sheridan's comedy *The Critic* (1779) called Whiskerandos. The word was occasionally substituted for whiskered in the form whiskerandoed.

Whiskerateur: a word invented by Frank Richardson, in his *Whiskers and Soda*. It means an amateur, or lover, of whiskers.

Whisker-bed: the face.

Whiskerette: a curl of hair hanging down over a woman's cheek.

Whiskers:
● the generic nickname for a whiskered man, the equivalent of Beardie. It was also American slang at one time for a federal agent. In more recent times applied specifically to a narcotics agent. There is an oblique reference to Uncle Sam.
● sometimes used as a slang word for whisky. 'Have some more whiskers, Brad, it'll do you

good,' says one character to another in Iris Murdoch's *The Black Prince*.

Whisker-splitter: 18th-century English slang for a womanizer, a frequenter of prostitutes. Beard-splitter was used in the same sense rather more frequently.

Wig beard: a false beard which has hair worked on a gauze or net foundation.

Wind tormentors: American tramp slang for a heavy growth of whiskers.

Wing: a moustache of the toothbrush type, but with sloping sides.

Zapata: a thick, Mexican moustache, made widely known in 1952 by Marlon Brando in the film *Viva Zapata!* Emiliano Zapata (1879–1919) was a Mexican revolutionary of almost pure Indian blood. He recruited an army of Indian peasants and led a revolution which on three occasions took over Mexico City. To the Mexican Indians he was a saviour and a hero; to others he was a bandit. (See page 99.)

And now for the rest . . . here are some other names that have been applied to different beards and moustaches by various writers.

à la Souvaroff (W), Alfalfa* (B), Artichoke leaf (B), Barbed wire* (B), Belgrave (B), Bellarmine (B), Besome-beard, Bigote (M), Billy goatee* (B), Boulanger (B), Bristles* (B), British beard (M), Brush* (B), Camberwell fringe (B), Chinchillas* (B), Christ's cut (B), Clark Gable (M),

Circular (B), Collier (B), Cookie duster* (M), Cork moustache (F), Cotelettes (W), Crates (W), Crop (B), Cross-over beard (F), Curl (M), Cutlets (W), Dewey (M), Droopy (M), Earguards (W), Enobarbus (B), Face furnishings, Fantail (B), Farmer Giles (B), Finger bleeder (B), Fer a cheval (B), Foliage* (B), Fool's (B), Fuzzy puss* (B), French fork (B), Galways (B), Gash beard, Greek (B), Grock (M), Guard-dagger whiskers (B), Hearthrug* (W), Hindenburg (M), Hoare-beard, Holbein (B), Hulihee (B), Jumbo Junior (B), Lambrequin (W), Ligue (B), Merkin (M), Moss* (B), Mouse-eaten (B), Musketeer (B), Muzzler* (B), Natal (B), Newgate knocker (B), Nokomis (B), Norris Skipper (B), Ovid (B), Paris (B), Pelot (W), Philosopher's (B), Picked beard, Pin (B), Plutonian (B), Punto (B), Raleigh (B), Reverend (B), Royal whiskers (B), Russian (B), Satyric tuft (B), Scotch beaver (B), Shrubbery* (W), Spanish cut (W), St James (B), Stash* (M) Stoic (B), Three-pointed (B), Throat whiskers, Trojan (B), Turkish (W), Weathercocks* (B), Whey beard, Wind chimers* (B), Zaken (B), Zits* (FB)

(guide: B – beard, F – false, M – moustache, W – whiskers, * slang)

A 1890s advertisement for moustache fixative.